Basic Writing

Essays for Teachers, Researchers,
and Administrators

Edited by

Lawrence N. Kasden
J. Sargeant Reynolds Community College

Daniel R. Hoeber
Mercy College of Detroit

National Council of Teachers of English
1111 Kenyon Road, Urbana, Illinois 61801

To Peggy and Maria

NCTE Editorial Board: Paul Bryant, Thomas Creswell, C. Kermeen Fristrom, Rudine Sims, C. Ann Terry, Robert F. Hogan, *ex officio*, Paul O'Dea, *ex officio*

Book Design: Tom Kovacs, interior; V. Martin, cover

NCTE Stock Number 02689

© 1980 by the National Council of Teachers of English. All rights reserved. Printed in the United States of America.

It is the policy of NCTE in its journals and other publications to provide a forum for the open discussion of ideas concerning the content and the teaching of English and the language arts. Publicity accorded to any particular point of view does not imply endorsement by the Executive Committee, the Board of Directors, or the membership at large, except in announcements of policy, where such endorsement is clearly specified.

Library of Congress Cataloging in Publication Data

Main entry under title:

Basic writing, essays for teachers, researchers, and
   administrators.

   Bibliography: p.
   1. English language—Rhetoric—Study and teaching—
Addresses, essays, lectures. 2. English language—
Remedial teaching—Addresses, essays, lectures.
3. English language—Teacher training—Addresses,
essays, lectures.   I. Kasden, Lawrence N., 1947-
II. Hoeber, Daniel R.   III. National Council of
Teachers of English.
PE1404.B3   808'.042'07073   80-14634
ISBN 0-8141-0268-9

Contents

Acknowledgments   v

1. An Introduction to Basic Writing   1
   Lawrence N. Kasden

I. The Basic Writer

2. A Look at Basic Writers in the Process of Composing   13
   Sondra Perl

II. Successful Basic Writing Programs

3. Basic Writing at J. Sargeant Reynolds Community College   35
   Arthur L. Dixon

4. Basic Writing Programs of the Western North Carolina Consortium   45
   Milton G. Spann
   Virginia Foxx

5. A Writing Laboratory Model   63
   Patrick Hartwell

6. The Rhetoric Program at Boston University's College of Basic Studies   74
   Harry Crosby

III. Evaluation and Testing

7. A Successful Placement Test for Basic Writing   91
   Nancy W. Johnson

8. Choosing or Creating an Appropriate Writing Test   105
   Rexford Brown

IV. Training Basic Writing Teachers

9. Training Teachers of Basic Writing 119
   Constance J. Gefvert

10. Staffing and Operating Peer-Tutoring Writing Centers 141
    Kenneth A. Bruffee

V. Research Opportunities and Resources

11. Research in Writing: The Issues 153
    E. Donald Hirsch, Jr.

12. Selected Bibliography: Composition and Basic Writing 164
    Daniel R. Hoeber

    Notes 174

    Contributors 184

Acknowledgments

No endeavor as large as publishing a book is done without the help of many people. This is certainly true in the case of this collection of essays. We would like to thank the many people who advised and encouraged us in this endeavor, especially Paul O'Dea, NCTE Director of Publications, Gary Tate, and members of the NCTE Editorial Board. We also realize that without the encouragement given us by our own institutions, it is not likely that we could have completed this work. For this encouragement we thank J. Sargeant Reynolds Community College President S. A. Burnette, Provost Thomas Overby, and Humanities Division Chairman Richard Brewer. We also thank Sister Karen Werra, director of the Developmental Service Program, Mercy College of Detroit.

We owe particular gratitude to those who did much of the typing and mailing of correspondence that were necessary to bring together these essays. For this assistance we thank Helena Beaman, Robin Cantor, and the many secretarial students who worked in the J. Sargeant Reynolds Word Processing Center and their teachers, Jo Ann Sherron and Jane Williams.

1 An Introduction to Basic Writing

Lawrence N. Kasden
J. Sargeant Reynolds Community College

In addition to discussing the purpose and content of the collection, the first chapter makes a case for basic writing courses based upon a thorough understanding of the nature and needs of the students for whom these courses are designed.

Although researchers and policy makers in government and education have only recently begun to pay close attention to developmental education, such basic instruction has existed at least since Wellesley College started a developmental program in 1894. Since that time the emphasis in programs for poorly prepared students shifted in the 30's to study habits, in the 40's to reading, and in the 60's to the underachiever's total personality.[1]

Today, research in basic or developmental education is widespread but not very systematic. Roueche and Wheeler point out that there are dozens of different terms to describe "catch-up" programs. They attempt to distinguish the two most frequently used terms, *remedial* and *developmental*:

> "Remedial" implies the remediation of student deficiencies in order that the student may enter a program for which he was previously ineligible. Typically, such work consists of noncredit courses in English, mathematics, or study skills taken as prerequisites to credit courses. "Developmental" or "compensatory," on the other hand, refers to the development of skills or attitudes and may not have anything to do with making a student eligible for another program. Under these latter approaches, curricular materials are frequently modified to begin credit work where the student is, and the academic calendar is modified so that the student can move at his own pace in acquiring mastery of a course.[2]

Cross believes that these terms should be used according to the aims and objectives of the program rather than according to the "pedagogical sophistication" of the approach. She notes that "a more useful distinction is to be found in the *purpose* or goal of the program":

> If the purpose of the program is to overcome *academic deficiencies,* I would term the program remedial, in the standard dictionary sense in which remediation is concerned with correcting weaknesses. If, however, the purpose of the program is to develop the diverse talents of students, whether academic or not, I would term the program developmental.[3]

Cross concludes that "remediation in academic skills areas is . . . a legitimate part of developmental education."[4]

Cross's classification system is especially useful. It acknowledges the need of some students for remediation in specific academic disciplines as well as the need of other students for cohesive enrichment programs that not only provide instruction in individual academic disciplines, but also assist the students to better understand themselves, to overcome adverse personality traits and those features of their environments that may interfere with their learning, and, finally, to absorb and integrate all that they learn about their environment, about their various subjects, and about themselves.

The works of Bossone, Cross, Gordon, Mulka and Sheerin, Coleman, Roueche, and others give us a fairly consistent picture of developmental students and the characteristics that may relate to their limited educational achievement.[5] Cross notes that low academic achievers often display five principal characteristics, although not all students who are in need of a developmental or remedial program display each of these: (1) poor study habits, (2) inadequate mastery of basic academic skills, (3) low academic ability or low IQ, (4) psychological motivational blocks to learning, and (5) sociocultural factors relating to deprived family and school backgrounds.

This list is at least partially supported by other research findings. Mulka and Sheerin, for example, note that "students from families in the bottom quarter of income have less than one-third the chance of students from families in the top quarter of completing an undergraduate degree."[6] Katz notes that low achievers are characterized by their great self-criticism and unfavorable self-evaluation.[7] Jaffe and Adams report that the "students' academic self-image has a stronger effect on college entrance than socioeconomic status" and that students who combine high grades with high self-image or low grades with high self-image are less likely to drop out of college than students who combine high or low grades with low self-image.[8]

Although attempts, especially at the community college level, have been made to assist students from low socioeconomic status groups, Folger states that such status is still a significant factor in determining academic success and that "paradoxically, the community colleges appear to have increased college opportunities for low-status youth, and at the same time, to have increased the socioeconomic differential in college completion."[9] While much is being done through federal and state programs to enable socially and economically disadvantaged students to meet the financial requirements of attending college, little has been done to help them overcome other barriers that appear to impede their educational progress. In fact, Gordon notes that our educational systems continue to inhibit minority and disadvantaged students even while they are in primary grades. Gordon and Wilkerson write that "many students from low-income and minority group populations are diverted from the academic stream as early as third or fourth grade by archaic tracking procedures."[10] Consequently, Gordon argues that for disadvantaged students to have a fair opportunity to earn college degrees, the colleges must offer developmental courses.

In addition to overcoming financial and educational obstacles, disadvantaged students must also struggle with social forces and expectations that work against their achieving educational success. Astin cites research studies indicating that the disadvantaged are less motivated and have lower academic and vocational aspirations than do people of higher socioeconomic groups and that this is often due to their realistic perception that for them there are few personal and vocational opportunities.[11] The relevance of these findings to a discussion of developmental education is made obvious by Roueche and Kirk, who note that the disadvantaged student, in particular, has low self-esteem. Such a student feels powerless, alienated, and incapable of coping and adapting.[12]

The barriers caused by poor self-image and low aspiration that characterize many developmental students cannot be dealt with simply. The students need assistance from the college so that they can overcome the environmental and parental influences that inhibit their chances for success. The assistance given by the college needs to be substantial and requires a substantial commitment, for schools are not exercising sufficient influence in these areas to have any meaningful effect. Coleman notes that at present

> schools bring little influence to bear on a child's achievement that is independent of his background and general social context; and that this very lack of an independent effect means that the inequalities imposed on children by their home, neighborhood, and peer environment are carried along to become inequalities with which they confront adult life at the end of school.[13]

We see, then, that to Cross's list of characteristics common to low achievers we might add such specific items as (1) lack of parental encouragement, (2) minority and/or sex discrimination, (3) occupational rather than academic preparation in the high school curriculum, (4) lack of motivation, (5) poor self-image, and (6) sense of powerlessness over oneself and one's environment. While these items characterize most basic writing students, it is by no means certain that they necessarily cause poor academic performance. We must also be especially careful not to assume that all or even most basic writing students are members of minority groups. According to Cross, "the overwhelming majority of low achievers who gained admission to colleges through open-door policies were *not* ethnic minorities. They were predominantly the white sons and daughters of blue-collar workers."[14]

Developmental Education

A comprehensive developmental education program must address many student needs. It must provide students with adequate financial assistance; it must improve their self-image and motivation; it must help them take responsibility for and control of their own lives; it must improve their study habits; and it must compensate for inadequate mastery of basic academic skills.

Helping students develop basic academic skills is very complex, for not only does it presuppose that the earlier stated needs are being met, but it requires faculty with expertise in a number of academic disciplines. The two principal skills of most developmental programs are mathematics and language arts. The language arts skills usually include reading, writing, speaking, and listening, but the language arts teachers must also be knowledgeable in dialectology and sociolinguistics, in psycholinguistics and learning theory, in phonics and articulation, and in the teaching of English as a Second Language (ESL). Writing teachers, for example, find their work is closely related to and often partially dependent upon students' customary manner of viewing and speaking about their environment, their ability to read, their vocabulary, and their experience in developing their thoughts. A cursory examination of just a few of the elements that the writing teacher must be concerned with may serve to suggest the complexity of teaching developmental writing.

The most respected and comprehensive study of teaching developmental writing is Shaughnessy's *Errors and Expectations*, which outlines the various writing problems developmental students have and the ways in which she and others have worked with these students. (Because of the significance of this text and Shaughnessy's other works, her term *basic* is most often used by English teachers in place of the more common terms *developmental, remedial,* or *compensatory*.)

Shaughnessy divides her study of writing problems into chapters on handwriting and punctuation, syntax, common errors, spelling, vocabulary, and units of writing larger than the sentence. In each chapter she outlines what the basic writers she has worked with know and do not know and how their lack of knowledge in one area affects their performance in others. For example, she notes in the chapter on handwriting and punctuation that basic writers have only tenuous command of the use of periods, commas, and capitals and almost no familiarity with the correct use of colons, semicolons, parentheses, hyphens, dashes, ellipsis points, and brackets. As a result, they cannot use parentheses and dashes to overcome the "linearity of sentences," they cannot use the colon as a means of economically presenting a series, nor can they use punctuation to provide a "map" that signifies to the reader the relationships, changes and continuity of their thoughts.[15]

Most basic writing teachers have firsthand experience with such writing. In fact, it is not uncommon to find in the writing of a single student many of the problems Shaughnessy mentions, as these samples from two students at my college indicate:

> Cars are a lot of trouble. My car for instance, when I friest bought it, I had No ideal that it cost me so much money to keep it up. (in shape) number 1, thier was the tititle to be change from the proprietor to me.
> Secondly, thier was licence plates that was needed for the car. thirdly, insurance that was also dafinitely needed. Also city stikcer, all which was costly and just the beganning of car trouble.
>
> A person's car tells what kind of person he is just like his home, but the up keep of it the cleannees the time you take with it wheather its run down or kept up well. If you car is always dirty on the out and in side people will figure you are the same way dirty out side and down in your heart, a car tells alot about a person life and what kind of persons he really is if your car is . . .

Shaughnessy says that these writing problems are not the result of ignorance of the relationship between the parts of a written composition, but from students' unfamiliarity with the standard conventions for showing those relationships.

Although oral drilling and speaking exercises are often helpful in teaching students to write, there are significant differences between oral and written codes. Many of these differences are discussed in Hirsch's *The Philosophy of Composition,* and the basic writing student's reliance on the oral code at the expense of writing is discussed in Ong's "Literacy and Orality in Our Times."[16] The works of linguists such as Labov, Shuy, and Wolfram substantiate Shaughnessy's claim that the speech of minority and disadvantaged students is grammatical, although not necessarily in agreement with conventions of either spoken or written standard dialect.[17] The issue of standards and correctness frequently arises when one works with basic writers, especially if they are from isolated rural areas or are minority students, as, for instance, when one examines the way some nonstandard speakers show time, person, and number. As we know, the rules in many nonstandard dialects make it unnecessary to use multiple linguistic markers to signify a single semantic item. (Thus, in some dialects there is no need to add an *-es* ending to the verb *go* in "The boy goes to the store" since the *-es* inflection serves only to repeat linguistic information—that the subject is third-person singular—already contained in the word *boy*.) We have learned that frequently the nonstandard writer and speaker is not incorrectly applying grammatical rules, but rather is often using a different set of rules. How the student can best learn to use the standard set of rules requires knowledge of fields outside the traditional training of English teachers, who generally do not have the requisite knowledge of linguistics, language development, and the methods used in teaching English as a Second Language.

Approaches to the Teaching of Basic Writing

The essays that follow directly address the concerns of basic writing teachers and those who teach basic writing teachers. The essays focus on program design and evaluation, teacher training, and research. Most of the basic writing courses described in the four essays in Part II allow students to concentrate only on those areas of writing with which they have difficulties. Most of these writing programs rely to some degree on the students' native competencies and intuitions about language; consequently, the programs often emphasize exercises that require the students to read their writing aloud, listen to it, and then edit with both eyes and ears. Some of the programs also put into practice, either consciously or not, Bloom's mastery learning theory: clearly stated objectives, a hierarchy of skills, and flexible schedules that allow students to spend as much time as it necessary meeting rather high performance criteria.[18] The lessons and writing assignments in these programs tend to be short, always beginning at a level that assures the student initial success. Students usually progress through the lessons at their own pace, often doing individualized or individually assigned lessons, and always receive an immediate response from the instructor. The students work much more closely with their instructors than is typical of other college courses, and the instructors, consequently, have additional opportunity to provide encouragement and support. Given what we know about basic writing students—their background, aspirations, and self-concept—it is clear that a close instructor-student relationship is necessary.

Others of the programs described do not attempt to separate writing into a set of subskills, but rather teach writing as a holistic process. In programs like the one described by Hartwell, students learn the subskills as they are needed in the process of their composing. As Hirsch notes in his essay in Part V, research has yet to verify which of these two approaches—teaching writing as a sequence of skills or teaching it as an organic process—is more sound. Hirsch hypothesizes that it is likely that both approaches are partially correct. It is possible that the best approach, based on careful analysis of the types of writing problems the students have, may vary from institution to institution, from class to class, from student to student. Based on the methods found to be successful in the programs described in this collection, however, it appears that students who have severe difficulties with standard dialect, usage, and sentencecraft may best learn by studying one element at a time, while basic writers who have fewer problems may better profit from a more organic approach.

Perhaps the most significant feature of all the basic writing courses described here is the requirement that students do an extraordinary amount of writing. Unlike the traditional freshman composition course, the basic writing course usually requires that students write daily. And even a lesson that concentrates on mastery of only one feature of writing usually concludes by requiring that the student demonstrate mastery by writing a controlled paragraph or theme.

Knowledge of course structure alone, however, will not insure that a basic writing teacher will succeed, since much of the content one needs to know to teach basic writing is not what most writing teachers study in their graduate programs. For such teachers and, even more so, for teachers of future teachers of basic writing, Gefvert's essay in Part IV provides a guide through the most recent theories and findings regarding those areas of basic writing that deal with interference and surface features as well as composing as a process.

While the types of writing problems that warrant the concern of the basic writing teacher at one school may primarily, or at least most immediately, be surface ones—syntax, grammar, standard dialect—at another school the basic writing teacher may start a course with more rhetorical concerns, such as organization, development, coherence, audience, and style. Such concerns are the principal focus of one of the three courses described by Spann and Foxx and the courses described by Hartwell and Crosby. These are also the primary concerns of Bruffee's article on training peer tutors. Like the other writers, Bruffee emphasizes the importance of accessibility, flexibility, individual instruction, and frequent and prompt response and encouragement. Furthermore, he describes a rigorous program for training peer tutors that can be readily adapted for effectively training full-time teachers of writing.

The essays by Johnson and Brown in Part III discuss writing assessment. Johnson argues that student-written essays provide the best basis for placing students in the proper writing course. However, as many of us know, the time and cost involved in administering and grading such placement essays often make using them unfeasible. As a less satisfactory but nonetheless fair and reliable alternative, Johnson recommends a carefully constructed objective test of the students' knowledge of writing skills. Brown reviews the types of tests basic writing teachers and administrators may use and the purposes each type serves. Like Johnson, Brown cautions that no test can serve all purposes and that care must be used in selecting a test instrument.

The second essay of the collection describes some of the characteristics of student writing. Perl's essay focuses on the writing process used by some basic writers and the differences between this process and the composing process of more skilled writers. She notes that even in the process of writing, these students are often insecure, frequently stopping themselves, constantly checking for errors, and uncertain as to the direction in which to head. Perl notes that basic writers so frequently interrupt themselves in the composing process to correct surface features that they lose track of their thoughts; thus, their writing is often incoherent and disjointed. In response to this habit of basic writers, a teacher can either have students ignore surface problems in order to concentrate on composing and hope they will master the standard code through greater exposure to good reading and writing, or the teacher can help students master the standard code first so that they do not interrupt their composing unnecessarily. Which of these instructional approaches is more viable is uncertain, but it may, again, very much depend upon the degree to which students' composing is interrupted by such surface features. Of course, any actual instructional program will include something of both methods, and we can best judge the effectiveness of a program by looking at the writing the students produce.

We should remain aware of the importance of research and the valuable service it provides classroom teachers. Students will not master basic skills simply because their teachers are sensitive and empathetic or ethnically or culturally similar. Of paramount importance is the teacher's knowledge of the subject matter and his or her ability to impart that knowledge. Hoeber's concluding bibliography provides ready access to much of the present body of research on composition and on basic writing specifically, and Hirsch's article suggests further areas that need to be researched carefully so that we can accumulate a verifiable body of knowledge that can be readily built upon.

Prospects of the Discipline

The initial intention of this collection was to bring together views of people who had earlier spoken or written about different aspects of basic education and teaching writing. We expected the essays to cover the wide range that they do, but we are, quite frankly, surprised at the degree to which the various essays reinforce one another, build upon common principles, and provide an assuring sense that teaching basic writing is a discipline. The disagreements, too, are reassuring, for they remind us that there is still much to be learned.

Beyond these reasons there is a very practical justification for this collection: while teaching positions in English diminish in number, more and more people are being hired to teach basic writing. The number of tenure track positions in composition and rhetoric has grown rapidly, and in 1976 the Modern Language Association found it necessary to establish a separate job classification called "developmental English."[19] Worth writes that "to the extent that college teachers are wanted at all, there is a market of sorts for teachers of composition and reading, and for persons able to work with students most of whom would never have gone beyond high school until very recently."[20]

As teachers of basic writing, we have come through the first stage of our own change. We have become accustomed to meeting in our classrooms students who, as Bruffee notes, "could not, or would not, write sentences in a way that made sense to us," who "did not think as we thought," who "did not value what we valued," and who "misconstrued what we had asked them to do in ways that were beyond our ability to comprehend."[21] We have recognized and attempted to rectify our lack of knowledge and our shortcomings as teachers of writing. In the process we have come to recognize the complexity of the task students are asked to accomplish and the virtues and sophistication of the resources they bring to it. As a result we are better able to respect, support, and encourage our students. Only more complete knowledge will better enable us to teach them.

I The Basic Writer

2 A Look at Basic Writers in the Process of Composing

Sondra Perl
Herbert H. Lehman College, CUNY

> Perl uses the writing process as a means of understanding the prewriting habits of basic writing students. The information gained through her study reveals much that modifies our current views of the basic writer and ought, therefore, to modify the instructor's methodology in working with the basic writer.

For over one hundred years American colleges have offered courses in written composition, but only in the past ten years have researchers begun to study how people write. It was not until 1969 that Emig showed that composing—the procedure through which writers put words on a page to form a text—is amenable to research and warrants the concern of all writing teachers. Her pioneering work on the composing processes of twelfth-grade students was followed in 1973 by Graves's work on the composing processes of seven year olds.[1] By raising pertinent questions on process, Emig and Graves inaugurated a new direction in the field of written composition: the study of the actions through which written products take form.

Emig recognized that the lack of knowledge concerning the nature of the composing process placed composition teachers on shaky pedagogical grounds. As she put it:

> If certain elements in a certain order characterize the evolution of all student writing, or even most writing in a given mode, and very little is known about these elements or their ordering, the teaching of composition proceeds for both students and teachers as a metaphysical or, at best, a wholly intuitive endeavor.[2]

Using a case study approach, Emig examined the composing processes of eight twelfth-grade students who ranged in skill from adequate to highly proficient. In order to aid her in discovering what students do as they write, Emig used a tape recorder and instructed her students to "compose aloud," that is, to verbalize whatever thoughts crossed their minds while they were writing. The eight students in her study engaged in this "specialized form of verbal behavior"[3] on two occasions. During two other sessions they discussed with her particular pieces of writing completed between sessions and memories of their previous writing experiences.

As a result of her study, Emig identified ten dimensions of the composing process that had rarely been given the attention she believed they deserved: the context of writing, the nature of the stimulus, prewriting, planning, starting, composing aloud, reformulating, stopping, contemplating the product, and the influence that teachers of composition seem to have on their students' writing.[4] She found that her students engaged in two dominant modes of composing, the extensive and the reflexive, each mode being "characterized by processes of different lengths with different clusterings of components":

> Reflexive writing has a far longer prewriting period; starting, stopping, and contemplating the product are more discernable moments; and reformulation occurs more frequently. Reflexive writing occurs often as poetry; the engagement with the field of discourse is at once committed and exploratory. The self is the chief audience—or, occasionally, a trusted peer.
>
> Extensive writing occurs chiefly as prose; the attitude toward the field of discourse is often detached and reportorial. Adult others, notably teachers, are the chief audience for extensive writing.[5]

Emig's findings led her to challenge many of the current assumptions and practices of writing teachers. She pointed out that while extensive writing is the mode favored by most teachers, reflexive writing receives more sustained interest from students. This, she suggested, accounts in part for the "limited, and limiting,"[6] writing experience of most secondary school students. Furthermore, Emig concluded that teachers of composition "underconceptualize and oversimplify the process of composing."[7] Her work stands as the first attempt to alert teachers to the many intricacies that begin to emerge when attention is given to the composing process.

In 1973 Graves investigated the writing processes of seven-year-old children. He analyzed the themes that appeared in the writing of ninety-four children, observed the behaviors and strategies of fourteen children while they were writing in either "formal" or "informal" classroom settings, and focused particular attention on eight children, reporting one as a case study. Based on his observations of how children write, Graves divided his seven year olds into two types, each exhibiting distinctive characteristics. According to Graves, *reactive* writers are those who need immediate rehearsal in order to write, who use overt language to accompany writing, who proofread at the word level, and who lack a sense of audience. *Reflective* writers are those who rehearse minimally before beginning to write, who compose silently for the most part, who reread periodically at the word or phrase level, and who have a growing sense of their audience.[8]

In addition to these and other specific findings, Emig and Graves established important methodological precedents for future research. They showed that detailed, systematic observation is possible through a case study approach. Their work demonstrates that case study research can provide the rich, albeit tentative, findings that will help generate new theories and hypotheses amenable to testing and analysis. In the remainder of this article I will report findings from my own work in which I used the case study method to examine composing processes among basic writers.[9]

Overview of the Study

The research reported here addressed three major questions: (1) How do basic writers write? (2) How can their writing processes be analyzed? and (3) What does an increased understanding of their processes suggest about the nature of the composing process in general and the manner in which writing is taught in the schools?

I chose to study unskilled writers in a community college for two reasons. First, students whose writing is judged as "deficient" in language skills and whose linguistic and educational backgrounds set them apart from the better-prepared, traditional college students are a growing segment of the college population. Second, such students have been most seriously constrained by the traditional approach used to teach writing, the "product orientation" that focuses on the errors of performance without acknowledging the writing competencies that lie beneath the surface.

An underlying assumption in this study was that an adequate understanding of a human process will most likely develop from observing people while they engage in that process. Observation alone, however, is not enough. A systematic method for reporting what has been observed is also crucial. In this study I devised a coding system for describing and analyzing what students do as they write. This method provided a way of viewing on one page the movements and behavioral sequences of a student's composing process; a way of determining the frequency and duration of each behavior; and a way of assessing the relation of each behavior to the whole process. Using this coding system,

I constructed a composing style sheet for each student. Study of the style sheets revealed the patterns of a student's process; these patterns allowed me to determine similarities and differences among the group of students.

The College

The study took place during the 1975-76 fall semester at Eugenio Maria de Hostos Community College of the City University of New York. Established in 1970 and deliberately placed in one of the most economically depressed areas of New York, the south Bronx, Hostos Community College was designed with a dual purpose: to handle the excess of new students expected to enroll at the City University as a result of its newly instituted open admissions policy and to serve the needs of the urban poor who inhabit the Bronx ghettoes. The students who attend Hostos are nontraditional college students, impoverished both by economic circumstances and a lack of sound educational experience.

The Students

In order to represent a range of educational background and experience and yet remain within reasonable case study limits, I selected five students for this study. One was a Puerto Rican male, twenty-one years old, who had dropped out of high school to join the U.S. Marines and was now hoping to improve his economic situation by getting a college education. Two, a male and a female, were Jamaican students who had come to this country for high school and had stayed on to attend college; and two were black American females, one a recent high school graduate living at home, the other a twenty-seven-year-old high school dropout with four children of her own. All represented the first generations of their families to attend college.

The students had been placed into the Libra program at Hostos, an interdisciplinary basic skills program designed to link college-level "content" courses with basic-level reading and writing courses.[10] All of the students were native speakers of English. All tested below the 10.0 grade level on a nationally standardized reading test (see Table 1), and all of their placement essays exhibited the "writing deficiencies" associated with basic writers: "an inability to organize, poor diction, commitment of gross errors in grammar, and an inadequate knowledge of punctuation and mechanics."[11]

Since Libra ia a "block" program, all students in this study had identical schedules and attended the same classes. Furthermore, through my deliberate choice, all of the students in the study were members of my writing class. I made this choice for two reasons. First, by selecting my own students for the research, I would know firsthand what they were studying in their content courses and thus would be able to construct topics for the writing sessions that legitimately reflected classroom work. Second, from working with, relating to, and getting to know my students in the daily, interactive manner that enhances teaching, I would most likely develop the rapport and trust necessary for case study, process research. I decided that these considerations outweighed the need to justify claims of "objectivity," since creating the customary distance between subject and observer may have made it virtually impossible to conduct the study at all.

I introduced the study to the students during class time and presented it as a collaborative effort between the students and the teacher. I explained that although teachers try to "teach writing," they don't really know how individual students actually compose and that one of the only ways to discover this is to observe students in the process. The study, I concluded, would be one in which the students provided the means by which teachers would learn more about their task. All fifteen students in my class volunteered for the study with the understanding that there would be five sessions, each taking place outside of class time. None of the five students selected missed any of the sessions. Although there was no mention of remuneration, once the data collection was complete, I paid the students for their time and participation.

The Design

I met with each of the students for five individual one-and-a-half-hour sessions. Four of the sessions were devoted to writing and one to an open-ended, in-depth interview concerning the student's perceptions and

Table 1

Reading Scores: California Achievement Test, Level 5

Student	Vocabulary (Grade Level)	Comprehension (Grade Level)	Total (Grade Level)
Tony	9.7	10.1	9.9
Dee	10.5	7.6	8.9
Stan	10.0	9.8	9.9
Lisa	6.6	7.8	7.2
Beverly	7.0	8.2	7.6

memories of writing and writing instruction. When time permitted, I questioned students at the end of each of the writing sessions on their perceptions of their own writing process and on the choices they made while writing. All of the sessions took place in a soundproof room in the college library, and all sessions were tape recorded. (See Table 2 for particulars of individual sessions.)

Composing Aloud

Customarily, people compose to themselves. As a consequence, most of what goes on during this process is hidden from an observer. In an attempt to bring to light the patterns and movements that occur during composing, I followed Emig's example in directing the students to compose aloud, to verbalize as much as possible whatever they were thinking from the time they received the topic to the time they considered themselves finished. I realized, as did Emig, that nobody can say everything that comes to mind. So students' verbalizations cannot be taken as anything more than a rough approximation of events that remain

Table 2

Design of the Study

Session	Mode	Topic	Directions
1	Extensive	Society and Culture	Students told to compose aloud; no other directions given.
2	Reflexive	Society and Culture	Students told to compose aloud; no other directions given.
3	---	Interview: Writing Profile	---
4	Extensive	Capitalism	Students told to compose aloud; also directed to talk out ideas before writing.
5	Reflexive	Capitalism	Students told to compose aloud; also directed to talk out ideas before writing.

largely internal and ineffable. It is also conceivable that asking studen to compose aloud changes the process substantially, that composin aloud is not the same as silent composing. These and other methodo logical issues can only be settled through further research.

The Topics

All of the students in this study were enrolled in a course entitled "Introduction to Social Science," which I attended as part of the basic writing program. The topics chosen for sessions one and four of my study were drawn directly from the material presented and discussed in the social science class and were typical of the impersonal, formal assignments required in college courses. The topics chosen for sessions two and five referred to the same general material but asked the students to take a personal approach. The general topics were "Society and Culture" for sessions one and two and "Capitalism" for sessions four and five. It should be noted that before sessions one and two took place, the terms *ideology* and *cultural beliefs* were discussed in class, along with the American principle of equal opportunity. Similarly, prior to sessions four and five, classroom discussion focused on the rise of capitalism as an economic system. Antecedents to capitalism were explained as well as its concomitant problems. Thus, the concepts and the vocabulary used in the phrasing of the topics in this study should have been familiar to the students. The topics and their sequence were as follows:

Session 1

Topic: Society and Culture [Extensive]

Directions: Answer the question below by relating it to class discussions, readings, and your general knowledge of the problems of New York City. Give examples to illustrate your ideas, but remember that you are being asked to write about the general problems of New York City and their effect on the *society* as a whole, not on your personal life.

Question: All societies have ideological beliefs. One of the ideologies of American society is that all men are created equal. In what sense is this cultural belief being threatened today by the financial crisis of New York City?

Session 2

Topic: Society and Culture [Reflexive]

Directions: During this session, you are being asked to write on your personal thoughts and feelings about a particular American belief. You may handle the topic in any way you like, but remember that you are being asked to relate the topic to your personal experience.

Question: All societies have ideological beliefs. One of the ideologies of American society is that all men are created equal. If this is true, then you and the members of your family are equal to everyone else in America. Describe your personal reaction to the last statement and define what "being equal" means to you.

Session 4

Topic: Capitalism [Extensive]

Directions: Discuss the following statement based on your readings, class notes, and your general knowledge of American society.

Statement: Define capitalism and explain how it operates in America today.

Session 5

Topic: Capitalism [Reflexive]

Directions: Answer the following question using as many details or examples from your life as you like.

Question: Do you believe in the American capitalist system? Why or why not?

The following are examples of student writing produced in response to each of the topics:

Dee
Session 1

In own Society today, it is said that all men are Created Equal. Now they are forced to look at a Financial Crisis. This will Probably Effect the black man in our Society more than anyone Else. Because he has alway had to work harder than anyone else to get What he Wanted. If the statement all men are Created Equal is ture, then why soul Should he have to Work harder to get on top. The white man I don't like that this I don't think the Financial Crisis is going to Effect that White man as much as the black man, because the White man can get over by the color of his Skin. Most People Come to New York Wh With the idea New York is where the money is at. Well the money is here, but Who Know Where? These people also believe that You Can get an Equal Chance for a job if you have a Education. Well I guess that part of it is probably ture. Now that New York is having a Financial Crisis these People Won't be able to get jobs Wheather they have a good Education or not. These people Came from the Environment where they grew up because they Wanted to find a Stronger Culture and perhaps Start all over again, Now these people will probably look at New York as a place what their biggest B biggest dreams were lost.

Lisa
Session 2

I don't believe that equality is being practist to the fullest in American Society today. American Society may say that everyone is equal. But they don't practial or treat everyone equal. Being equal means that every anyone can buy land, property, or live anywhere they want to if they can pay the asking price. regardless of sex, color, or creed. It also means each individual has the same rights as another within the laws. But I must admit things are better then they were years ago. Years ago when American Society talked about equality that ment for only certain class of people. Blacks couldn't buy land are live where they wanted to. There were a separation in towns Whites lived in big fine houses and had the best. But Blacks had to live in rundown houses which they didn't own. And had to work very hard in fields for what they got. Today things haven change but they are a lot better. It could still use some improvement. Sometimes we still can't live in the so call better area of the city. Even if you have the money. This not only goes for housing but Jobs as well. Do you know how it feel to walk into a place to buy something or to ask a question and the looks even the way they answer or their maner of speech tone you get. It's degrading. But I think that Blacks P.R. or any nationality should be treated or has the same right to live or go where they pleace. I think we contributed a lot to this country. We should be given equal opportunity just as much as the next man.

Stan

Session 4

Capitalism which is very well portrayed by the story of the "Man from Venis" shows the way in which he makes is living by trading goods from other lands and making a huge profits. Now it as the years prolonged countries were coping this principle. England became the major figure in Capitalism. This idea spread like wild fire that today America shows a great deal in Capitalism. Today it has been modified by rising surpluses and increasing the production. Alexander, Gimbles and Macy are making an abundant amount of profit based on the idea that if you take the surplus from the production and return it by uer p replacing either man or machine the production will increase. e.g.: If one man was baking 50 loveas of bread per day and receaves a payment of say two loveas a day. There Then the employer hiried/s another baker at the say same wages/the employer would be getting an increase of 96 loveas a day instead of 48. This is the principle which America is using today.

Tony

Session 5

I believe in America capitalist system because it is the only way of life I know. What I know from the one other system, for example communism. I would pef perfer to live in a capitalist system, for in a capitalist system you have the oppurtunity to get ahead /if you have the ability. In America they offer you the oppurtunity asto get the ability through education. Where as in in a communism country, if you have the ability they do not offer you the oppurtunity to get ahead. Because it is ran under dictatorship, which dictates that all are equal. This is not true /for many reason. Here is just one general example with the dictator of a communism country. + The dictator is always going to live better than his dictatees along with his friends, and family. I would not be able to live in a system/where I am told how to live.

Findings

A major finding of this study is that all five students displayed consistent composing processes: the behavioral subsequences prewriting, writing, and editing appeared in sequential patterns that were recognizable across writing sessions and across students. While the tone, the mood, and the specific content of each session differed, the data show that each student employed certain strategies in order to write—and that structurally the unfolding of these strategies occurred in discernible and stable patterns.

This consistency suggests a much greater internalization of process than has ever before been suspected. Since the written products of basic writers often look arbitrary, observers commonly assume that the students' approach is also arbitrary. However, just as Shaughnessy points out that there is "very little that is random . . . in what they have written,"[12] so, on close observation, very little appears random in *how* they write. Basic writers have stable composing processes which they use whenever they are presented with a writing task. While the consistency argues against seeing these students as beginning writers, it does not necessarily imply that they are proficient writers. Indeed, their lack of proficiency may be attributable to the way in which premature and rigid attempts to correct and edit their work truncate the flow of composing without substantially improving the form of what they have written. I will review in greater detail my observations and conclusions in the following subsections that treat the three major aspects of composing—prewriting, writing, and editing.

Prewriting

Prewriting played a minimal role in the composing processes of the students in this study. Time spent prewriting ranged from 1.5 to 7 minutes, with an average time of 5.5 minutes. During this brief time, these students used three principal types of planning for developing their ideas on a given topic:

1. Rephrasing the topic until one word or an idea in the topic connects with the student's experience. This establishes a connection between the student as writer and the field of discourse. The student

Basic Writing in the Process of Composing

then has "an event" or "an experience" in mind before writing begins.

2. Narrowing down the topic through dichotomizing or classifying. This breaks the large conceptual category in the topic (e.g., equality) into two manageable pieces for writing (e.g., rich vs. poor).
3. Focusing on a key word in the topic, initiating a string of associations to that word, and then developing one or more of the associations during the writing (e.g., equality → justice → criminals → murder → control of guns).

When students' planning proceeds in any of these ways, they begin to write with a sense of direction. Often they recognize that the act of writing itself may change some of their initial formulations and that these will have to be reworked on subsequent drafts. To the extent that such an understanding was clear to them, these students were similar to more proficient writers. However, basic writers rarely maintain this initial sense of flexibility and distance once rewriting occurs.

A fourth type of planning behavior also occurred at times during prewriting. Students read the topic a few times, indicated that they were not sure what they wanted to write, but stated that they would "figure it out" as they went along. In these instances their first sentence was often a rephrasing of the question. Then, after this first sentence was down on paper, planning began. Through composing aloud, they projected what they thought ought to come next and in this way clarified what they wanted to write about. After the clarifying took place, they moved back to writing and alternated between planning and writing throughout most of the discourse. This anticipatory planning or projecting ahead to determine what will come next appeared frequently during the writing itself, even after students had begun writing with a secure sense of direction.

Little time was thus spent on prewriting. But this does not mean that planning necessarily suffered. The strategies commonly associated with prewriting, such as planning and devising possible approaches to the topic, occurred even more frequently and with even greater effect upon the subsequent production of discourse once writing had begun. One might be tempted to conclude, therefore, that students begin writing prematurely and that the planning and clarifying of what they want to write ought to come first.

In contrast to such a conclusion, however, the data here suggest that certain strategies, such as creating an association to a key word, focusing in and narrowing down the topic into manageable pieces, dichotomizing, and classifying, can and do take place in a relatively brief span of time. The data also suggest that the developing of and planning out of ideas receive impetus from students' having already translated some of their ideas into written form—in other words, through the act of seeing their ideas on paper, students are enabled to reflect upon them and to develop them further.

Writing

Careful study revealed that the students wrote by shuttling back and forth from the sense of what they wanted to say forward to the words on the page and back from the words on the page to their intended meaning. This back-and-forth movement appears to be a recurrent feature that may be characteristic of composing even among skilled writers. At one moment students are writing, moving their ideas and their discourse forward; at the next they are backtracking, rereading, and digesting what has been written.

Occasionally sentences were written in groups and then reread as a "piece" of discourse; at other times sentences and phrases were written alone, repeated until the writer was satisfied or worn down or rehearsed until the act of rehearsal led to the creation of a new sentence. In the midst of writing, editing occurred as students considered the surface features of language. Often planning of a global nature took place: in the midst of producing a first draft, students stopped and began planning how the second draft would differ from the first. Often in the midst of writing, students stopped and referred to the topic in order to check if they had remained faithful to the original intent, and occasionally they identified a sentence or a phrase that seemed to produce a satisfactory ending. In all these behaviors, they were shuttling back and forth, projecting what would come next and doubling back to be sure of the ground they had covered.

These basic writing students exhibited a number of other back-and-forth strategies when they became "stuck," or when the words on the page seemed to them not to convey the meaning they intended. The most common strategy was to return to the topic, to read it again, to see if anything in the topic could regenerate the thought process that had been lost. A second strategy was to reread whatever was down on paper with the hope that through rereading, previous thinking would be retraced and the missing connection would emerge. Occasionally students sidetracked themselves with editing concerns, worrying over spelling, syntax, or punctuation, as though a "delaying" action on the surface level might provide time for connections to emerge from the deeper, meaning level. A final strategy was to delete what was on the paper and to begin again in another direction.

A number of recurrent operations were also initiated in the time between drafts. This time was always distinct, and no student in the study ever moved immediately from the first draft to the second. During this period, attending to the question occurred frequently, as did reading the discourse as a whole. The sense and flow of the writing were also considered, some areas were reworked and reworded, decisions about paragraphing and organization were made, and editing operations were performed.

Writing the second draft frequently took longer than writing the first draft due to the number of editing operations performed by the students. The majority were changes in form, but students also considered questions of vocabulary, style, organization, and audience. Students moved back and forth between drafts, repeating phrases from one, adding elements to another, exhibiting a continuous stream of encoding and decoding behaviors. Even when students composed silently, they paused frequently, added and deleted words, and rescanned in order to see what they had accomplished thus far.

Ceasing to write is always a definable moment. It occurs when students put down their pens and comment, "I'm finished," or "That's it." Yet, however and whenever the moment occurs, assessing what internal decisions led up to it is difficult. The students in this study often ceased to write because of physical constraints—their "hands are tired"—or because of mental fatigue—they had "run out of ideas." Summarizing or concluding statements were often tacked onto the discourse, but most of these statements did not seem to grow out of the flow of the discourse itself; rather, they seemed like appendages with a clear purpose but an impaired function—they preached rather than summarized, asserted rather than concluded, flatly stated the initial premise rather than pointed to further implications. At other times students tacked statements of opinion onto their discourse as if the act of stating what they believe absolved them from the task of developing their answers any further. All of these strategies point to the fact that students conclude the writing act as gracefully as they know how, but that their conclusions have more the quality of exits than endings.

A number of conclusions can be drawn from the observations of these students and from the comments they made. Although they produced inadequate or flawed products, they nevertheless seemed to understand and perform some of the crucial operations involved in skillful composing. While it cannot be stated with certainty that the patterns they displayed are shared by other writers, some of the operations they performed appear sufficiently sound to serve as prototypes for constructing two major hypotheses on the nature of composing in general:

1. Writing does not occur in a straightforward, linear fashion. The process is one of accumulating discrete bits down on paper and then working from those bits to reflect upon, structure, and then further develop what one means to say. Writing can be thought of as a kind of "retrospective structuring"; movement forward only occurs after one has some sense of where one wants to go. Both aspects, the reaching back and the sensing of forward movement, have a clarifying effect.

2. The development of meaning through writing always involves some measure of both construction and discovery. Writers construct their discourse inasmuch as they begin with a sense of what they want to write. This sense, as long as it remains implicit, is not equivalent to the explicit form it gives rise to. Thus, a process of constructing meaning is required. Rereading or backwards movements become a way of assessing whether or not the words on the page adequately capture the original sense intended. Constructing simultaneously affords discovery. Writers know more fully what they mean only after having written it. In this way the explicit written form serves as a window on the implicit sense with which one began.[13]

Editing

For the students in this study, editing occurred almost from the moment they began writing (see Table 3). It had a separate and distinct place in the time between drafts, it occurred again with generally greater frequency during the writing of the second draft, and it could be seen again, although in a diminished form, in the final reading of papers.

During editing, students are concerned with a variety of items: the lexicon (i.e., spelling, word choice, and the context of words), the syntax (i.e., grammar, punctuation, and sentence structure), and the discourse as a whole (i.e., organization, coherence, and audience). Changes in form greatly outnumber changes in content and, indeed, the students in this study spent a tremendous amount of time and energy on the correction of surface features of their writing. Spelling, an area that teachers will often neglect, received the most attention, while verbs, the one area that many teachers of basic writers traditionally emphasize, received the least.

An analysis of the content changes reveals that all of the students in the study concerned themselves with the depth, the fullness, and the style of their finished products. The following list summarizes the kinds of content changes made by the students:

1. Elaboration of ideas through the use of specification and detail (Tony, Dee, Stan, Lisa, Beverly)
2. Additions of modals that shifted the mood of a sentence (Tony)
3. Deletions or rephrasings that narrowed the focus of a paper (Tony, Stan)
4. Rephrasings that created a stronger opening (Stan, Lisa)
5. Clause reductions or embeddings that tightened the structure of a paper (Tony)
6. Vocabulary choices that reflected a sensitivity to language or an increased sense of audience (Tony, Dee, Stan, Beverly)
7. Reordering the elements in a narrative (Tony, Stan, Beverly)
8. Strengthening transitions between paragraphs (Tony, Beverly)
9. An awareness of and a concern for metaphoric language or ironic intent (Stan, Lisa)

Despite the sophistication of the content changes and the magnitude of the changes in form, a cursory look at any of the students' written products reveals that many problems remain unresolved. The problems in what may be called form included errors in syntax, punctuation, spelling, word choice, and sentence structure; the problems in what is traditionally called content concerned audience-speaker relationships, coherence, and the establishment of logical, consistent relations.

All of the students proofread their writing in order to make it conform to the code of standard written English and all of them concerned themselves with various aspects of style. These unresolved problems must therefore be accounted for by looking beyond the kinds of changes the students made to some of the problems that arose during editing. The following seven items summarize the problems for the students in this study:

> They frequently asked themselves, "Is this sentence [or feature] correct?" but they did not seem to have recourse to a workable set of rules to guide or inform their editing decisions. In searching for a "rule" or attempting to devise a principle that could be applied to the construction at hand, they often made changes that impaired rather than clarified their meaning.

> They seemed to have internalized a limited set of rules for correcting their own writing but they lacked recourse to all of the exceptions to the rule or extenuating circumstances that change the rule. As a result, they applied a rule where it did not belong and produced a hypercorrection.

They produced structures that were syntactically more complicated than the single set of editing rules at their disposal; when they tried to apply a rule to a complicated construction, they became tangled in their own syntax.

They had begun to experiment with "academic" language and to employ terms they were familiar with through class discussions or through other speech contexts; yet they were not familiar with the syntactic and semantic constraints one word places upon another, which led them to produce "lexical transplants" or "syntactic dissonances"[14] that jar readers familiar with these constraints.

They tried to rely on their intuitions about language, in particular the way words sound. Often, however, they had been taught to mistrust what "sounds" right to them, and they were unaware of the particular features in their speech codes that may need to be changed in writing to match the standard code. As a result, when they attempted corrections by sound, they became confused and began to have difficulty differentiating between what sounds right in speech and what needs to be marked on the paper. At times they attempted to rely on absolute sound-letter correspondences, perhaps because no one had ever told them that the way words sound depends primarily on context and particular language habits.

When they reread their papers with the intention of correcting errors, they read from a semantic or meaning model in their heads. They extracted the meaning they wanted from the minimal cues on the page, but did not recognize that outside readers would find

Table 3

Editing Changes

	Tony	Dee	Stan	Lisa	Beverly	Totals
Total number of words produced . .	1,720	1,271	1,640	1,754	2,179	8,564
Total form	210	24	49	167	100	550
Additions	19	2	10	21	11	63
Deletions	44	9	18	41	38	150
Word choice	13	4	1	27	6	51
Verb changes	4	1	2	7	12	26
Spelling	95	4	13	60	19	191
Punctuation	35	4	5	11	14	69
Total content .	24	7	13	2	21	67

these cues insufficient for meaning. In other words, although these students reread, they did not read closely or with analytic distance. They immediately imbued surface features with the meaning they *wanted* them to have without scrutinizing those features carefully to see if they carried such meaning "on their own." They exhibited a "lack of visual acuity with words and letters, a habit of seeing which swiftly transforms what is on the page to what is in the mind of the writer."[15]

Their writing was egocentric, understood as a cognitive psychologist uses this term. While they occasionally indicated a concern for their readers, they more often took the reader's understanding for granted. They did not see the necessity of making their referents explicit, of making connections among their ideas apparent, of carefully and explicitly relating one phenomenon to another, or of placing narratives or generalizations within an orienting, conceptual framework.

A number of conclusions can be drawn from the editing behaviors of the students in this study:

All of the students edited, and the nature of their concerns was remarkably sophisticated—far more sophisticated than one would suspect from a quick reading of their papers. Why their papers have so many unresolved problems has less to do with their being careless or "not editing" than it does with the rule systems they have only partially mastered, their selective perception, and egocentricity.

Editing for these students intruded so often and to such a degree that it broke down the rhythms generated by thinking and writing, forcing the students to go back and, when possible, recapture the strands of their thinking once an editing operation had been completed. Thus, editing occurred prematurely, before students had generated enough discourse to approximate the ideas they had; as a result, the students often lost track of their ideas.

While editing during writing occasionally has the effect of a delaying action which allows students to consciously focus on the surface features of language while they are waiting for ideas to be generated or to reach a level where they may be grasped, editing also has the effect of side-tracking, of busying students with the more superficial aspects of writing and thereby drawing them away from the real problems inherent in composing—constructing and discovering meaning. Here editing becomes a strategy for avoiding writing.

Editing is primarily an exercise in error-hunting. The students were prematurely concerned with the "look" of their writing; thus, as soon as a few words are written on the paper, detection and correction of errors replaces writing and revising. Even when they began writing with a tentative, flexible frame of mind, the students soon became locked into whatever was on the page. They had not yet developed the same flexibility or suspended judgment in editing that they had developed in planning and writing, a flexibility essential to revising that, when done successfully, allows writers to juggle possibilities and rework ideas.

The Mode of Discourse

One of the questions in this study was whether the mode of discourse—extensive or reflexive—would affect the students' composing processes. While students do not always acknowledge that a particular mode is specified and while they occasionally switch from one mode to the other during writing, the following observations regarding the effect of mode upon their writing processes can be made:

The basic writing students in this study were more fluent in the reflexive mode, consistently producing more words with greater ease and generally in less time. Their writing pace was smoother and characterized by fewer pauses and hesitations. Sentences were often written in groups, with one sentence flowing easily from the preceding one. In this mode students also expressed approval of their written products more frequently and indicated they had some sense of how they wanted their papers to end.

Composing in the extensive mode was characterized by more pauses and hesitations. The hesitations occurred both within individual sentences and, more frequently, between sentences. Thus, sentences were often written in isolation, and the students' attention was often focused on individual words rather than on the larger units of discourse. The pace of writing was sporadic; students reread often, and they had many false starts and negative assessments. They frequently returned to the question, were consistently stuck in one place, and exhibited difficulty moving forward with their ideas. As a rule, fewer total words were produced in this mode even when the total composing time exceeded that given to the reflexive mode.

Since students do not always remain in one mode during writing, the greater ease and fluency associated with the reflexive mode may need to be accounted for by a further analysis—one that may have less to do with what students are actually writing about and more to do with how the topic for writing and the initial directions for writing set a particular tenor and tone. It may be that students develop their ideas with greater facility when they are addressed directly, as in the reflexive mode. When a distance exists between them and the topic, as it does in the extensive mode, the distance itself and the wording of the directions may make access to their ideas more difficult. Thus, students may need a wedge, or a "way in," to the topic. When this is provided, as it is by the personal nature of the reflexive mode, extensive or reflexive writing may occur smoothly. When this wedge is less apparent, as it often is in the more distanced, abstract directions of the extensive mode, writing of whatever nature may be more difficult.

Conclusions

Basic writers have traditionally been viewed as students who "do not know how to write." The data in this study reveal, contrary to common opinion, that basic writers have stable composing processes. They have definite strategies to start, sustain, and stop writing, and the composing behaviors these strategies set in motion occur in a consistent fashion. Indeed, one of the reasons the writing of these students remains flawed is related to the nature of the behaviors set in motion during composing. Seen from this point of view, teaching basic writers how to write needs to be conceived of in a new way, in part, by "loosening" the process rather than "tightening" it.

One possible way to loosen the process, or to free students from some of the constraints under which they presently write, is to provide them with guidelines that draw on an experiential model of the composing process. This model would need to explain the kinds of processes set in motion when writers write in such a way that students, during the act of writing, could begin to assess where they are, what they are doing, and what they need to do next. Such a model emerges in the following outline of the four features of the composing process. As features, rather than steps or stages, the four are interwoven or alternating strands of the overall process itself.

(1) Readying oneself for writing. Drawing from one's experience a sense of what one wants to write about; coaxing what one means to the surface through words; making the commitment to write by moving from the initial sense of one's meaning to a readiness, however tentative, to go in a certain direction with one's ideas; and starting to write.

(2) Sustaining the flow of writing. Having begun to write, keeping the flow of thoughts moving; keeping hold of the thoughts long enough to translate them into written symbols and get them down on paper; cultivating backward movements to check where one has been and forward movements to project where one wants to go; developing the writing in this recurrent manner and keeping track of possible alternate directions.

(3) Shaping the discourse for oneself. Reading one's writing to determine whether the words on the page correspond to one's intended meaning; getting the writing "right" with the "self," recognizing that there is a "writing self" and that by matching the meaning of what one thinks to what one writes, one can clarify meaning further; reworking and refining the writing so that it more precisely conveys what one wants to say.

(4) Readying the discourse for others. Reading and reworking one's writing in order to meet the demands of readers; distancing oneself from the written product in order to assess whether readers unfamiliar with the context will be able to follow one's thinking; editing one's writing so that surface features of the written code will not distract readers from their primary focus—the extracting of meaning from the written page.

The students in this study acknowledged and integrated the processes of these four features with varying success. Some they performed naturally; others they had learned and performed mechanically; others they still need to learn. Frequently, however, the ones they performed mechanically interfered with their developing and sustaining others.

Using the term *basic* to refer to the writers in this study is thus apt. It is not that these students "do not know *how* to write," for they enact many basic composing processes and exhibit many of the strategies of more practiced writers. Their problem is not one of absence but of emphasis. This lack of knowledge is not surprising. Having been drilled on the surface features of language, they focus prematurely on form. Having learned how topic sentences should lead to proper paragraph development, they are uncomfortable when the sequence of what they write is not clear and does not conform to the models of polished discourse in the textbooks. While these writers lack an understanding of some of the rules governing the form of clear and forthright prose, more importantly they lack an adequate conception of what they are being asked to do when their teachers tell them "Write."

II Successful Basic Writing Programs

3 Basic Writing at J. Sargeant Reynolds Community College

Arthur L. Dixon
J. Sargeant Reynolds Community College

Dixon describes a sequential basic writing program with emphasis on the organization, instructional techniques, and the day-to-day workings of a program which has produced excellent results at the two-year college level.

A few years ago one might have started an article like this with an anecdote about a traditional English teacher confronted for the first time with what are variously called nontraditional, basic writing, remedial, or developmental students. An essential feature of the anecdote would have been the teacher's shock at seeing the kinds of language problems he or she was expected to deal with. But by now, few English teachers have not had to deal with such students and such problems. It can be a frustrating experience, sometimes a rewarding one, but always a challenging one. This article will describe one method for teaching basic writing using easily available materials. The method is flexible and provides for frequent one-to-one contact between student and teacher, a necessary condition for the effective instruction of most basic writing students. Further, the course requires neither hardware nor special facilities (though tables are better than tablet chairs) and is no more expensive than traditional courses except that enrollment should be limited to no more than fifteen. The course does not turn all those who take it into good writers, but it has proved helpful in preparing most of them for college-level work.

All freshmen entering J. Sargeant Reynolds Community College take a writing placement test developed at the college. It consists of correcting ten "sentences" containing errors and writing a paragraph at least ten sentences long on one of a number of suggested topics. The ten sentences in the first part contain the most common kinds of errors made by students who are traditionally diagnosed as remedial: subject-verb disagreements, nonstandard forms, fragments, and run-on sentences. Failure to find and correct the errors in three or more sentences is a first indication that the student may need developmental work. However, because some students can correct errors in isolation but cannot produce consistently correct forms in their own writings, the paragraph is a better indication of skills and can either confirm or reverse the preliminary judgment made on the basis of the sentences.

Experienced English teachers can read and come to holistic decisions about placement paragraphs very quickly and with impressive consistency.[1] The English Department at J. Sargeant Reynolds conducted an experiment with the placement test by having all the full-time English teachers read the same ten tests and decide whether or not the students needed developmental writing. Some tests fell into a borderline class; in these cases the grading teacher would seek another reader for the test before making a decision. The consistency of the whole faculty was approximately 85 percent and the chances of placing a student correctly were 91.5 percent.

The Basic Writing Course

The Verbal Studies Laboratory, the basic writing course at J. Sargeant Reynolds, meets five hours a week, and the students work individually, with the teacher providing supervision and tutoring. The course has four units: basic grammar, standard grammar and usage, sentence combining, and paragraph writing. All students in the course do the first unit, largely as homework, and, on the basis of a diagnostic test similar to the placement test, start their classroom work in one of the other units. Thus, most students begin their classwork with standard grammar and usage or with sentence combining. Since the basic writing course is primarily aimed at problems at or below the sentence level, only rarely is a student placed in the course for composition problems beyond the sentence level.

For many students, the basic writing course takes two or three quarters to complete. Students who have not completed the course but who are making satisfactory progress get a grade of R (re-enroll) at the end of each quarter. Those who complete the course get a grade of S (satisfactory). The course carries five credits which do not count towards graduation but do count towards a full load for financial aid purposes.

Basic Grammar

For students and teachers to discuss sentences and words productively, they must share a basic vocabulary, and the first unit of the course helps provide that. To introduce students to standard grammatical terminology, or to remind them of the terminology they learned in elementary or high school, all students in the course work through a programmed grammar text, Joseph C. Blumenthal's *English 2600* (New York: Harcourt Brace Jovanovich, 1973). The text begins with the identification of subjects and verbs and goes through sentence patterns, modifiers, the sentence unit, subject-verb agreement, capitalization, and punctuation. There are twelve units in the text, and students must pass a test on each with a score of 80 percent or above. The text is fairly easy to use, and almost all students can learn the material on their own, needing help only with occasional problems. Tests are administered periodically, and the teacher can help individual students with material that the test results indicate they have not yet mastered. Students are retested on the material, using alternate versions of the tests, until they pass with the required score. Most students can do six to eight units per quarter. The programmed text units on fragments, run-on sentences, possessives, and the like can also be assigned by the teacher in response to particular problems the student may be having in other units of the course. While the knowledge of grammatical terminology alone does not improve students' writing, it does enable them to discuss their writing with their teacher and with other students—something that is essential for improving their writing.

Standard Grammar and Usage

The book used for the standard grammar and usage unit is Constance Gefvert et al., *Keys to American English* (New York: Harcourt Brace Jovanovich, 1975), a book intended for speakers of nonstandard dialects (called "community dialects" in the text), especially "Black English Vernacular."[2] The text puts the standard and nonstandard dialects side by side as each paradigm or form is discussed to help the student recognize the differences, an important but often difficult step in achieving "correctness." The text starts with the third-person singular -s and goes through all the basic inflectional forms of verbs that cause problems: third-person singular present tense, past tense -*ed*, irregular verbs, compound verb forms. There are also sections on noun forms (plurals and possessives) and syntactic forms (indirect statements, passive constructions), but the section on verbs is the one most useful to the majority of students.

The text is unlike most handbooks for writing because it includes scores of exercise items in each lesson. A lesson begins with the presentation and discussion of a paradigm, and then, using the type of extensive drill and pattern practice often employed in teaching foreign languages, it provides enough practice for the student to begin to internalize the standard forms. The first lesson, for example, provides eighty short sentences in which the student must identify the verb, decide if it should have the third-person singular -s, and write the correct form if the one in the sentence is wrong. Then there are seventy-odd sentences where the student must supply the correct form of a given verb. Finally, each lesson has a series of sentences, constituting a paragraph, to be proofread and corrected.

All of the lessons have the same basic format, so students need not learn new instructions with each lesson. This allows the students to move easily from lesson to lesson without having to wade through new instructions or depend upon the teacher for interpretation of directions. To further facilitate the student's progress and free the instructor, the English staff at J. Sargeant Reynolds has filled in all the correct answers in one copy of the book so the students can check their own answers after they have gone through a set of exercises.

By the time they have completed a lesson, most students have learned the material fairly well. Some students, however, continue to have trouble with some of the forms because of interference from the dialect they have grown up with and continue to use outside the class. As Shaughnessy and others suggest, our job as teachers of writing is to give the students the competence to write standard dialect, not necessarily to speak it; students may have to produce the standard forms consciously while writing or in proofreading, unlike the unconscious way they produce the forms of their first dialect or language.[3] Though oral production is not the goal of the course, oral drill can help students with some forms. It can help attune the student's ear to the difference between forms—for example, between a verb with an -s ending and one without—much in the way oral drill helps students of English as a Second Language recognize the phonemes of English. (Speakers of some languages do not hear the difference between the English words *ship* and *sheep,* for example. Because the difference between the vowel sounds in those words is not a significant feature of their native language, they must learn to hear the difference.)

In oral drill the teacher works with an individual student, specifying a verb and tense: *run,* let us say, in the present tense. Then the teacher leads the student through the present tense paradigm of the verb by giving cues that will elicit all the cases (e.g., *I, you, he, they, the girls*). The student responds by repeating the cue and adding the proper form of the verb. This kind of oral drill can be done rapidly and quietly, without disturbing the other members of the class. As I will discuss later in relation to sentence combining, the ability to "hear" what has been written is important to students' ability to proofread their work for errors in standard dialect.

The twenty-five lessons on verbs in *Keys to American English* are the ones needed by most students who have dialect-based problems with standard grammar. Students can be assigned particular portions of the remainder of the text—lessons on nouns, pronouns, adjectives and adverbs, questions, negatives, and sentence patterns—on the basis of a diagnostic test made by selecting items from the lessons in those parts of the text.

Since the course is self-paced, students progress at different rates through the unit on standard grammar and usage. Teachers must keep close track of their students' progress, encouraging them when they are having difficulties with some material and working orally and individually with them briefly almost daily. To show their mastery of the material, students take tests based on the material in groups of lessons. After lesson three, for example, the students take a ten-item test on the first three lessons, regular verbs in the present and past tenses. If the student gets eight of ten right, she or he goes on to the next group of lessons; a lower score means the student must go back through the material, with increased supervision by the teacher. Since the number of lessons in each group is kept small, most students pass most tests. This success, which the entire course is designed to provide by presenting the material in short segments, helps with student motivation and self-image, two keys to academic success.[4] Students who have resisted academic English for years because it baffled them or who have so seldom met with success in school that they hesitate to commit themselves to any academic task begin to see that they can deal with "English-teacher English." When they see that the rules of the standard dialect can be learned, they begin to feel they can learn it.

Most students who begin with the unit on standard grammar and usage will finish the first twenty-five lessons in a quarter. After that, and after they have finished any later sections in the text indicated by the diagnostic test, they go on to the second part of the course if their diagnostic test indicated need for work in sentence writing. Students who have command of standard forms but need work in sentence writing skip the first unit and begin in the second unit, sentence combining.

Sentence Combining

The second unit of the course is based on sentence combining, a technique intended to improve syntactic fluency by tapping the linguistic ability that all native speakers of the language possess. Originally developed in an attempt to use the theories of transformational grammar to improve student writing, sentence combining has been investigated by a number of researchers and has been shown to be an effective technique for improving the quality of student writing.[5] Though not generally used to teach correctness primarily, sentence combining can be so used when combined with instruction in grammar and punctuation of the sentence unit. Sentence-combining exercises temporarily free students from the need to invent and allow them to play with sentences, practicing patterns they can later use to express their own ideas. Foreign students who get into the basic writing course generally do not work in sentence combining because they do not have the intuitions a native speaker, even a speaker of nonstandard English, has about what is grammatically acceptable in English. Instead, they work with a controlled composition text.

The sentence-combining text we use is William Strong's *Sentence Combining: A Composing Book* (New York: Random House, 1973). Basically, students are asked to combine groups of short sentences into longer sentences. These groups become longer and more complicated as one progresses through the text, requiring more complex transformations to make good sentences. In the second part of the book, there are models to follow so that students can become familiar with particular structures, such as participial phrases and absolute phrases. Here is an example of the sentence-combining exercises from the first part of the book:

> The Nuremberg War Trials followed World War II.
> The trials posed a dilemma.
> The dilemma was for individuals.
> The individuals were thoughtful.
> The individuals were all over the world.
>
> = [1] The Nuremberg War Trials followed World War II and posed a dilemma for thoughtful individuals all over the world.
>
> = [2] The Nuremberg War Trials that followed World War II posed a dilemma for thoughtful individuals all over the world.

The following is one of the models from the second part of the book:

> The teacher smiled to himself.
> *The teacher erased the blackboard.* [base clause]
> The erasing was with a sweep.
> The sweep was lazy.
> The teacher trailed patterns.
> The patterns were of chalk dust.
> The chalk dust was gritty.
> The chalk dust was grayish.
>
> = Smiling to himself, the teacher erased the blackboard with a lazy sweep, trailing patterns of gritty, grayish chalk dust.

After the teacher explains the idea of sentence combining and does the first few combinations orally, students can generally do the next few orally without difficulty. As they work through the text, students try out their transformations subvocally, perhaps writing them out and trying several to find the one that sounds best, and then they write their final versions to hand in at the end of the class period. The teacher analyzes the combinations outside the class and goes over them with the student during the next class period. When the teacher hands the sentences back, he or she has the student quietly read aloud sentences that contain errors. The students will generally stumble at the points of error in the sentences, indicating their intuition that something is wrong, an important step in their learning to proofread their work with their ears, so to speak. As every English teacher knows, students will write things they would never say, would be all but incapable of saying; sentence combining helps transfer their usually accurate linguistic intuitions about correctness to their writing. Sentence combining also offers another advantage: most students do most sentences correctly, again helping to improve their self-image.

Because sentence-combining exercises result in comma splices and run-on sentences more than other kinds of errors, the teacher should explain these to the students individually as they come up. When errors of any kind occur, they should be taken up one at a time. The teacher may choose sentences with a particular kind of error for the student to read aloud. In addition to explaining the rules to the student, the teacher can direct the student to the relevant sections in the programmed grammar text.

In order to practice generating their own sentences, students should write at least one paragraph a week, based on one of the suggestions for writing in the sentence-combining text or topic assigned by the teacher. This aids in the transfer of the structures students are practicing to their own writing and keeps the exercises from becoming tedious. The transfer to writing of skills learned in sentence combining has been confirmed by numerous studies. It is worth noting that beginning with the Bateman and Zidonis study in 1966,[6] all the research with which I am familiar on the effects of sentence combining uses student-generated free writing, not sentence-combining exercises, to measure the changes induced by sentence-combining practice.

The sentence-combining text that we use serves the additional purpose of introducing the students to paragraph organization, since the exercises are arranged in groups that form paragraphs on various subjects. This has the effect of modelling discourse for students, one of the purposes of readers used in composition courses. By in essence rewriting dozens of paragraphs, students tend to absorb the concepts of paragraph unity, coherence, and development. It is not, perhaps, as rigorous a way of learning the rhetoric of the paragraph as traditional methods, but it has some of the same virtues.

As Shaugnessy suggests in *Errors and Expectations*, the errors students make in sentence structure are often the result of their ambitious attempts to do too many things in the same sentence. The orderly building up of complex sentences that sentence combining provides can help students tap and control the linguistic competencies they already possess and enable them to write ambitious sentences without too much mix-up. The following paragraphs illustrate some of the effects of sentence-combining instruction. The first paragraph was from the student's pretest, the second from her post-test.

> The main reason I have chosen special Ed. is to try to help those who are not as luck or as fortunate as you and me. There are alot of mental retarted people & children. Some people do not even care about them they just leave them a lone because they know that they can not get any better. I know that some children will never get any better but at least you can give them some kind of hope something they can hold on to. Even if it may be it is just to learn how to hold a pencil that is a big accomplishment for them and for me.

> The main duty of my job is to help people. I am a salesgirl so I am always working with people. I help them make decisions on what to get grandmother or what scarf goes with what dress. I also deal with merchandise, checking it in, making sure it is what we ordered and if not sending it back and last but not least working with money, clearing the register, helping trainees with the register and making change.

There are still some errors in the post-test paragraph, but it is syntactically much more mature than the pretest paragraph, and it has a satisfying rhythm and flow that are entirely absent in the pretest paragraph.

Paragraph Practice

Students begin to write paragraphs while they are working in sentence combining and write them exclusively in the last unit of the course. The text we use in this unit is called *Paragraph Practice*, but any set of paragraphs illustrating a number of paragraph development types would work equally well. In this unit students write ten paragraphs modelled on those in the text, which include sample instructions, descriptions, and exposition. This unit, usually the briefest in the course, gives students the chance to put together all that they have learned. In some cases, problems the student seemed to have mastered earlier in the course will reappear; in fact, new ones may appear. This gives the teacher the opportunity to have the student review particular items and reinforce them so that the student produces adequate work in regular composition courses. Errors can be expected to reappear from time to time under pressure and through carelessness. However, having gone through the material of the course, students are generally equipped to find and correct errors they may not even have been aware of before the course.

Teaching the Course

Much of the day-to-day handling of the course has been covered in the description of the way the students use the books. There are some practical matters that ought to be mentioned here, however. The first days of the course are devoted to diagnosis, a general introduction to the course, and a discussion of the importance of learning the standard dialect to succeed in college and in later life. The abritrariness of the prestige dialect is discussed, but most of the students know that they need to learn it if they are to do what they want with their lives and few have philosophical objections. The teacher describes the overall design of the course so that students know what they are supposed to do and learn. Attendance policies, grading policies, and the like are specified. Within the first few days, each student gets a form that shows what units of the course she or he needs to do, including a list of the tests so that the student will know when to ask for them.

Getting everyone started in the right texts is time consuming and sometimes less than perfectly orderly. Small groups of students are introduced to the texts and shown how to use them. At J. Sargeant Reynolds, in order to keep the cost of the course as low as possible for the students, the college provides copies of *Keys*; students who will begin with that unit usually start first. Students must purchase their own copies of *Sentence Combining* and *English 2600*. Since students starting in these books will not have their texts on the first day after diagnosis, they can be let go early on the day the other students are introduced to *Keys*. All students need some introduction to *English 2600* because the programmed approach is new to almost all of them and is confusing at first. This can be done for the group as a whole and then later for the small groups starting the units, since it takes a while for students to get the idea clearly.

Once the course is under way, with all students aware of what they are to do, the teacher's role becomes that of supervisor and tutor. When students in *Keys* are ready for particular tests, the teacher gives and grades the tests; *English 2600* tests are handled the same way. Students in *Sentence Combining* hand in the sentences they have done in class each day. The teacher goes over them outside class and then goes over them with the individual students in class, as described earlier. The teacher also goes over the paragraphs as they come in and discusses them with the students. Oral drills with *Keys* students, grammatical explanations for students in *Sentence Combining*, assigning topics for paragraphs, and generally keeping everyone working make up the rest of the work in the course.

All of this sounds like a lot of running from student to student, and it is; but once the class is under way, it goes fairly smoothly. Teachers cannot usually spend a great deal of time with each student, and sometimes it takes two days to get around to the whole class. Teachers must remember that they are supervisors, directors of the learning the students do on their own, and that they cannot teach everything.

Detailed records of each student's progress in the course—tests taken and passed, pages done in sentence combining, and types of errors and assignments made in response to those errors—are essential for the success of the course. Near the end of the quarter, students who are nearing completion of the course are given the exit test, another version of the placement test, so that they can register for one of the regular English courses if they are ready. Also, students the teacher thinks have learned enough to succeed in one of the regular courses may be encouraged to try the exit test. Finally, any student may challenge the exit test; since passing the placement-exit test is the measure of the student's readiness to enter the regular program, this seems only fair. To insure impartial and reliable grading, the exit tests are scored by another member of the English staff who does not know the status of the students whose tests are to be read. At the end of each quarter, the teacher fills out a form showing how far each student who does not receive an S grade (satisfactory) has advanced so that a new teacher the following quarter knows where the student needs to begin.

Results

No systematic follow-up of students who have completed the developmental course has yet been done, but the free writing students do by the time they finish the course shows a marked improvement in grammatical correctness, sentence structure, and style. Errors are not completely absent, but they are more like the errors one finds in any composition course, isolated and fairly infrequent. The Verbal Studies Laboratory course makes success in the regular composition courses possible for students who would stand very little chance in them without the practice and training it provides.

4 Basic Writing Programs of the Western North Carolina Consortium

Milton G. Spann
Appalachian State University

Virginia Foxx
Appalachian State University

The authors describe in detail the writing programs that have been individually designed by member institutions of the Center for Developmental Education for use at schools belonging to the Western North Carolina Consortium.

In August 1974, fourteen two-year institutions and two regional universities were incorporated under state law as the Western North Carolina Consortium. Prior to the incorporation, the member institutions had successfully worked together in such areas as curriculum, evaluation, faculty-staff development, and student services under the stimulus of a Title III grant from the U.S. Office of Education.

In 1975 Appalachian State University, a member of the consortium, and the W. K. Kellogg Foundation of Battle Creek, Michigan, engaged in discussions that revealed a mutual interest in the field of developmental and remedial education. Both parties perceived that, nationwide, increasing numbers of students were entering postsecondary institutions without the expected prerequisite skills, particularly the basic skills of reading and writing. The presidents of the consortium institutions were then asked by the chancellor of Appalachian State to consider a cooperative effort in the field of developmental and remedial education. A proposal was written, revised several times, and ultimately accepted by the foundation; funding followed in the spring of 1976.

The support given by the Kellogg Foundation and administered by Appalachian State's Center for Developmental Education has produced several developments that address the needs of academically underprepared adults. One of these developments has been the strengthening of existing writing programs and the initiating of new ones at consortium schools. We will discuss several of the more successful basic writing programs found at the three types of schools in the Western North Carolina Consortium: four-year public universities, community colleges, and technical institutes. Writing programs at one institution of each type will be described.

Catawba Valley Technical Institute

Catawba Valley Technical Institute, located in Hickory, North Carolina, has an enrollment of 2,500 full-time students. Since accepting its first student in 1960, Catawba has been committed to comprehensive education in a variety of occupational fields; it offers associate degree and diploma programs in business, allied health, engineering, furniture manufacturing, and environmental-agricultural occupations. Part of the commitment of the institution is to implement an "open door" admissions policy. Since 1965 Catawba has attempted to meet the needs of students with weak academic backgrounds through a Directed Studies Laboratory (Learning Lab), which provides assistance for students with deficiencies in reading, math, English, science, and numerous other subjects.

In addition to the laboratory, Catawba has, with varying degress of success, experimented with other techniques for teaching basic skills. The result of the experimentation is an innovative basic writing program, now in its sixth quarter of operation, which, according to evaluation, is successfully meeting its objectives. This basic writing course utilizes a language experience technique to improve communication skills. All four communication skills—speaking, listening, writing, and reading—are involved in the students' learning activities. The ultimate focus, however, is on written composition.[1]

Students are placed into the basic writing course if they score 21 or below on the English section of the Comparative Guidance and Placement Test (CGP). The course meets three hours a week for an eleven-week quarter and yields three hours of elective credit. Class size is limited to twenty students. The end-of-course objective is the same for every student: each individual must demonstrate competence in written communication by writing a paragraph at least one-half page in length which meets specific criteria in organization, unity, sentence sense, and usage. At the beginning of the course, diagnostic procedures determine the discrepancy between each student's current writing competence and the standard established for passing the course.

Diagnostic procedures include a writing sample, an evaluation of the student's sentence sense, and a test on recognition of common usage

Organization	Possible Points	Paragraph 1	Paragraph 2	Paragraph 3	Paragraph 4
Introduction	8				
Development	8				
Conclusion	5				
Total (Must be *15 or more*)					

Errors	Points Per Error	Paragraph 1	Paragraph 2	Paragraph 3	Paragraph 4
Fragment	8				
Run-on (fused) sentence	8				
Comma splice	8				
Comma in compound sentence	4				
Comma after introductory element	4				
Punctuation with inserted element	4				
Punctuation with add-on element	4				
Comma with parallel elements	4				
Weak sentence	4				
Apostrophe	3				
Verb tense	3				
Verb agreement	3				
Pronoun agreement	3				
Pronoun case	3				
Plural form of noun	2				
Adjective-adverb confusion	2				
Spelling	2				
Capitalization	1				
Other: _____	1				
_____	1				
Total (Must be *15 or less*)					

Fig. 1. Weighted scale for writing diagnosis.

errors. Diagnosis from the writing sample takes place through the use of a weighted scale (see Figure 1). Other diagnostic tests have been item-analyzed so that a specific test item error is known to indicate a need for work on a specific skill. Prescription charts similar to Figure 2 have been developed to facilitate the assignment of appropriate work.

Once students' needs have been tentatively identified, they receive an individually prepared assignment sheet appropriate to their current level of achievement (see Figure 3). Usually students undertake work on just one of the problem areas at a time (fragments, subject-verb agreement, etc.). When they can demonstrate understanding in this area, they write another composition to practice application of this new learning. As the course progresses, the students' prescriptions are adjusted in keeping with the instructor's observations of strengths and weaknesses in their writing. The repetition of this diagnose-prescribe-apply cycle results in substantial improvement of skills in a short period of time.

In this writing course, everything the student writes involves the four communicative modes of speaking, listening, writing, and reading. The

Problems	Books					
	Potter		Glazier		Young	
	Study	Exercises	Study	Exercises	Study	Exercises
Noun plurals	115-117	118			2	9
Noun possessives	147-148	148	26	28-31	3	11, 13
Pronouns Case Agreement	77-79 83	80 84	106	107-110	19 20	29 27
Verbs Principal parts Tense Agreement	35-37 31-32 47-49 51-53	38-44 33 50 54-56	99	102-105	37 38 40	49 45, 51 41, 53 57, 59
Multiple negatives	163	164			176	
Adjectives and adverbs	59-69	62 66 70-74			63	68
Words frequently confused	93-108	96, 100	6	10-13	155	161
Other						

Fig. 2. Prescription chart for supplementary books.

students *speak* what they want to say into a cassette recorder, then *listen* to what they have spoken and *write* it out—transcribing from their own dictation. Next, they revise what they have written, making changes and corrections as they see the need. They then *read* their written composition, again recording it on tape, and *listen* to this recording, making further revisions as they see fit. This cycle may be repeated as many times as is necessary until the students' compositions represent the best that they know how to produce. They then submit to their instructor the final drafts, along with all rough drafts and the casssettes on which they have recorded their work.

Outside class, the instructor reacts to the students' papers by speaking to each student via the cassette tape. At the next class session, the

	Assignment	Emphasis	Date Started	Date Completed
	Diagnostic Paper			
C1A	Oral paragraph[1]			
C1B	Written paragraph			
	Rx[2] _____			
	Sentence lesson[3] _____			
C3	Paragraph: Organization and unity			
	Rx _____			
	Sentence lesson _____			
	Paragraph: Your topic			
	Rx _____			
	Sentence lesson _____			
	Progress Paper			
C4	Paragraph definition			
	Rx _____			
	Sentence lesson _____			
	Paragraph: Your topic			
	Rx _____			
	Sentence lesson _____			
	Progress Paper			
C5	Paragraph description			
	Rx _____			
	Sentence lesson _____			
	Paragraph: Your topic			
	Rx _____			
	Sentence lesson _____			
	Progress Paper			

Fig. 3. Assignment Sheet for basic composition.

1. Letters and numbers refer to sections in Doris Clinard Weddington, *Patterns for Practical Communications: Composition* (Englewood Cliffs, N.J.: Prentice-Hall, 1976).
2. The *Rx* blanks are used to specify additional work from other resource materials.
3. Reference is to Weddington, *Patterns for Practical Communications: Sentences* (Englewood Cliffs, N.J.: Prentice-Hall, 1976).

students listen to the instructor's reactions and comments. Their papers, however, have not been marked; instead, the students must find their own errors and make their own revisions by listening to the instructor's hints, explanations, and editorial suggestions.

Instruction in the organization of written composition is provided through audio-tape lessons from Weddington's *Patterns for Practical Communications: Composition* (Englewood Cliffs, N.J.: Prentice-Hall, 1976). These materials teach a variety of organizational patterns needed for effective oral and written communication, focusing on real-life communication needs for home, community, and work situations. They also teach the student to use the speak-listen-write-read-revise cycle described above.

Instructional activities, which alternate with the writing practice, focus on sentence sense, punctuation, and usage and are drawn from a variety of sources. Any audio-visual or print materials could be used, provided the presentation is appropriate in its level of difficulty and the material is designed in such a way that the sections can be used in any order. Materials which have proven especially useful are Weddington's *Patterns for Practical Communications: Sentence;* Thomas's *Relevance of Patterns;* Potter's *Language Workshop;* Glazier's *The Least You Should Know about English;* and Young and Symonik's *Practical English.*[2]

All evaluations of learning are based directly on the student's writing. Evaluation is standardized through the use of a weighted scale, designed by faculty to reflect the values they place on each of a variety of specific competencies. Qualities such as organization, development, and unity are given positive numerical values. Points earned by the student are summed and must meet or surpass a minimum score for organization. Sentence faults and other errors such as punctuation, usage, spelling, and capitalization are assigned negative point values. The number of errors in each category is multiplied by the weight given that type of error; these values are summed for a score in mechanics. In this case, the accumulated point value must be equal to or less than an established criterion score.

The student's diagnostic writing sample is evaluated at the beginning of the course; the error counts and scores are recorded; at appropriate points during the course, at least three more papers are submitted and scored according to the weighted scale. The progress papers are separate from the practice compositions written as part of the learning cycles and are always produced without the aid of recording equipment. Some instructors ask each student to write a progress paper after the completion of every second composition-remediation-practice cycle.

Other instructors prefer to have the full class sit for these progress papers at regular intervals throughout the term.

The weighted scale proves useful not only in identifying needs and enabling prescriptive treatment, but also in motivating students to work toward improvement of skills. Students begin to realize that the errors marked on their papers in previous educational experiences were not, as they had supposed, just a mysterious scattering of criticism representing the teacher's feelings, but rather that these errors can be categorized into *types* of errors, some of which they tend to produce more frequently than others. The remark is often heard: "All I have to do is learn where to use capital letters, and I can cut my error points in half," or, "I can write a passing paper next time if I just learn to use a period instead of a comma between sentences." It is a common occurrence to have students *request* work in certain areas once they can see for themselves where their greatest needs lie.

The raw scores on the weighted scale can be converted into a grade in keeping with the institution's standard grading system. If the student reaches the minimum performance level before the end of the term, he or she continues to work for improvement. A student who has not reached the required proficiency level by the end of the term receives a grade of "incomplete" and continues to work until the necessary level of competence has been achieved.

The Catawba course has been evaluated by pre- and post-tests of competencies. Evaluation of improvement in skills and retention of students in the course are quite positive. One group of students reduced the incidence of major sentence errors by an average of 79 percent in four weeks (twelve class hours). An administration of the English section of the CGP before and after the course revealed that students in the language experience writing course gained ten percentile ranks on the average during the eleven-week quarter, increasing from 7th percentile to 17th percentile on national norms.[3] In the same eleven weeks, a traditionally taught grammar class showed an average improvement of three percentile ranks (12th percentile to 15th percentile on national norms). Attrition data show that 81 percent of the students in the individualized class successfully completed the course as opposed to 64 percent of the students in the traditional grammar group.

Student and faculty reactions are in agreement with these objective findings. Students give the innovative course a higher overall rating than the traditional grammar course. The language experience course ranked first out of six basic skills courses evaluated (including reading and math courses); the traditional grammar course ranked fifth. Instructors who have used the new techniques also express strong preference for this course over the traditional basic grammar. They feel that with these individualized language experience methodologies, their efforts are more effective in helping students learn to write.

Surry Community College

Surry Community College is located in the foothills of North Carolina in Dobson, the county seat of Surry County. The fall 1977 enrollment at Surry was 1,450 FTE students (the head count was 1,650). The majority of students attending are from within a fifty-mile radius of the school. In addition to a college transfer program, nineteen technical programs and four vocational programs are offered at Surry.

A special program for underprepared students was begun at Surry in 1972. In that year and the following two years, a total of forty-six students were enrolled in the program; since 1974, the program has expanded to serve approximately fifty students per year. The main elements of the program are as follows:

1. Credit is given for all courses.
2. Students are enrolled in special sections of reading, English, or mathematics depending upon their indicated areas of weakness (determined primarily from entrance tests). The main attempt to improve skills is carried out within these regular credit classes.
3. Students who have deficiencies in two or more areas (from among reading, English, and mathematics) are enrolled for the full Special Studies sequence.
4. In addition to the special sections of reading, English, and mathematics, students enrolled in the full Special Studies sequence take a prescribed set of courses during the first year. This set of courses includes study skills, speech, a human potential seminar, physical education, and social science electives.
5. Extensive counseling, both individual and group, is emphasized.

The developmental English courses at Surrey are designed so that students may work on their specific areas of weakness in basic English grammar and composition; just as important, students are able to work toward the completion of requirements for the college transfer English course. These two objectives were included in the course design because of past experiences with underprepared students. These experiences showed that with proper counseling, students acknowledged they were underprepared and needed remedial work in basic English skills; but when no credit was linked to their efforts, student motivation gradually decreased and attrition levels became unacceptable. It was also found that assigning students to a noncredit "precourse" in English further differentiated them from the general college population. This separation resulted in much negative feeling toward the course.

Current practice calls for all incoming students to be screened on the basis of their scores on the English section of the CGP. Those students who fall below a scaled score of 44 (30th percentile nationally, 11th locally) are advised to enroll in developmental English. Enrollment is not mandatory, but approximately 90 percent of those students so advised do enroll in the course.

In addition to the credit-earning aspect of the developmental courses, there are several key features which contribute to their overall effectiveness. First, students are tested with a locally designed pretest to determine areas of strength and weakness. Based on the pretest, individual prescriptions are made so that students spend time and effort only on areas where a weakness is evident. Each instructional module is self-contained, treats a specific skill or set of related skills, and is highly structured. The format of the modules allows students to work at their own paces. Post-tests have also been constructed for each module, and progress to subsequent modules is contingent upon mastery of the previous ones. Feedback on performance in the module exercises and module post-tests is immediate. Finally, assistance and instruction are constantly available from the instructor and student tutors. The ratio of tutors to students is approximately one to seven; the ratio of instructors to students is approximately one to twenty-three.

The individualized modules are the center of the instructional process. Each module is formulated to take students from deficiency level through the level required to meet requirements for a regular credit English course. Thus, remedial and regular credit work are incorporated into every instructional unit. Of the fifteen modules—eight in English 101 and seven in English 102—students must complete all those in which their course pretest score falls below 90 percent.

Each module contains an instruction sheet, materials and exercises, and the post-test. The instruction sheet specifies the objectives of the module, the procedures to be performed, and the standards for completion. Each module includes a variety of reading materials, practice exercises and audio materials. A significant aspect of every module is the provision of alternate learning materials and techniques. If, for example, a student is still having difficulty attaining proficiency in a certain skill even after completing the standard module, the student is provided with a different set of materials to accomplish these same objectives. After students complete the module activities, they are given the unit post-test. Several alternate forms of each post-test are available for retest purposes. Students are, however, encouraged to complete additional practice materials before taking a retest. Students are advised to achieve a score of at least 70 percent on post-tests before moving to the next module.

English grammar and usage are the emphasis for the first eight modules (English 101), with a gradual shift toward composition in the remaining seven modules (English 102). While the attention to grammar per se may run counter to current trends in English instruction, grammar was included so that the content of developmental courses would be comparable to the content of nondevelopmental courses at Surry. So far, indications are that the early emphasis on grammar is justified when students concentrate only on their specific areas of weakness, use individualized materials, and are made aware that their grammar skills will soon be employed in the development of composition skills.

English 103, which covers production of a formal research or term paper, is coordinated with English 101 and 102, but its instructional approach is quite different. Rather than using individualized modules, English 103 employs more traditional techniques in teaching students the procedures and skills involved in writing a research paper. Yet even in this course, several features are rather nontraditional. Following lecture-discussion sessions that cover the procedures and standards to be followed, class sessions move to the library. At this point, the library becomes essentially an individualized learning laboratory. The instructor and student tutors provide immediate and practical assistance to students in the use of library resources, the organization of materials, and the actual writing of the paper. Each stage in the production of a research paper is monitored, and corrections must be made before students move on to the next stage. Submission of papers is scheduled to allow ample time for revisions if they are needed. The structure of the course and the individual attention provided assure that most students are able to successfully prepare an acceptable research paper.

There have been two kinds of attempts to evaluate the effectiveness of the developmental courses at Surry. First, an objective measure of achievement during the course of one quarter in English 101 was performed by analyzing pre- and post-test scores on the English section of the CGP. Using data from thirty-five students, the average pretest score was 43.49 (26th percentile nationally), and the average post-test score was 46.17 (35th percentile nationally). A correlated t test revealed the difference of 2.68 points (9 percentile points) to be significant ($p <$ .05). An analysis of scores from a regular English comparison group revealed a nonsignificant increase during the course of a quarter, thus suggesting that the observed increase in the developmental course was not due to a test-retest phenomenon.

Additional analyses were conducted on student performance in the developmental course for the two following quarters (English 102 and 103). Again using scores on the English section of the CGP, results of two correlated group t tests indicated significant gains ($p < .05$) each quarter. The average pre- and post-test scores for each quarter were as follows: English 102, 46.13 (35th percentile) and 48.21 (40th percentile); English 103, 48.71 (45th percentile) and 52.00 (56th percentile). No regular English class comparison group scores were obtained for the second and third quarters.

A second evaluation procedure consisted of a student evaluation of the course. Using an instructor-designed questionnaire, students rated their satisfaction with various aspects of the course and the instructor. The results indicated very favorable attitudes toward the format of the course, the content of the modules, and the instructors. Students considered the self-pacing aspect of the course as very beneficial. The quality of tutor assistance and the availability of immediate feedback on performance in exercises and tests were also regarded very positively. Students also offered constructive criticism of some of the exercises in the modules.

Appalachian State University Programs

Appalachian State University has offered a range of special academic programs for students with skill competencies varying from remedial to honors since 1962. Due to increasing faculty and administration concern about the skills of entering students, the offerings in remedial-developmental courses have increased in the past few years. The English Department has provided two special remedial programs for students, the English Writing Laboratory, which has been in existence since 1964, and the Workshop in Composition, which was developed in 1976. In addition to these departmentally based programs, since 1973 the General College has sponsored the Special Services Program, a comprehensive counseling-academic program serving approximately one hundred underprepared students each year. One of the components of the Special Services Program is an interdisciplinary communications course, Introduction to Communications.

English Writing Laboratory.

The laboratory began in 1964 as a service to transfer students seeking teacher certification who, after completing a screening test involving the writing of a theme, were found to be deficient.[4] As the laboratory's reputation grew, the English faculty began referring other students to it, especially freshmen. By 1974 the laboratory had expanded to provide a university-wide walk-in service along with comprehensive support service for freshman English. In the early years, the laboratory was open four hours a week; it is currently open twenty to twenty-five hours a week.

Approximately two dozen students from areas other than English come to the laboratory during a given semester, spending up to twenty hours each. Referrals from English faculty number about seventy-five a term, and these students spend an average of twelve hours a semester in the laboratory working at their own pace. For these students, the work in the Writing Laboratory serves as a supplement to their regular classroom experience.

The Writing Laboratory is supervised by a full-time associate professor in the English Department who also teaches courses in composition and American Literature. Five to ten English graduate students are also employed each year to work an average of three hours a week. The instructor, graduate students, and materials are funded out of regular departmental funds. The additional personnel enable the laboratory to provide a high degree of personalized instruction to each student.

The laboratory has tutoring and instructional materials available for every course objective in freshman English.[5] (Objectives for the two semesters of freshman English have focused on sentence structure, basic expository writing, mechanical correctness, rhetorical forms, research, and literary analysis.) The classroom teacher usually designates the areas the student needs to review, usually by a note on the referral form the student brings to the laboratory. In addition, students are encouraged to bring in graded themes for use in tutorials.

While tutoring is preferred, commercial materials and materials prepared by members of the English faculty are used. The locally prepared materials cover in modular form proofreading and correcting major usage errors (fragments, run-on sentences, subject-verb agreement, pronoun-antecedent agreement, and verb forms), writing about literature, and writing a research paper.[6]

Workshop in Composition

This course was established by the English Department in 1976 for those transfer students in teacher education scoring below the 33rd percentile on the STEP Writing Test.[7] The course reviews basic composition and gives one hour credit. Each semester, forty to sixty students enroll in four sections of the course, which are taught by a faculty member in the English Department. Each class meets two hours a week; in addition, the instructor is available for consultation for four regularly scheduled conference hours every week. The course is graded on a satisfactory-unsatisfactory basis, an S being equivalent to a grade of C or better.

During the first week, students are asked to write an expository theme. If it is satisfactory, they are allowed to drop the course and are declared proficient in writing. If students do not exit the course in the first week, they must remain at least until midterm, at which time they may exit upon satisfactory completion of all assignments.

The focus of the course is the composing process. The approach taken is the one used by Donald Murray at the University of New Hampshire and Roger Garrison at Westbrook College. The Garrison-Murray approach emphasizes the establishment of priorities for writing and for proofreading. Using the following "editorial checklist," the instructor reads each paper, evaluating only one criterion at a time in the order listed below.

1. Specificity: use of detail, absence of vulnerable generalizations
2. Organization: statement of a thesis and evidence of a sense of direction
3. Expression: fluency, variety, and diction
4. Correctness: special attention given to five major errors (fragments, run-on sentences, subject-verb agreement, pronoun-antecedent agreement, and verb forms)

The student revises and corrects a paper until it is satisfactory in each area. Use of the checklist has contributed immeasurably to the efficiency and effectiveness of the one-to-one instruction during the tutorials and in conferences.

In summary, the course is organized around assignments presented via written materials which are prepared in advance, frequent consultation with students, and self-pacing. Course priorities are clear standards for writing and proofreading, tutoring and editing rather than lecturing and grading, constant writing and revising, and student accountability.[8]

Introduction to Communications

This course is an attempt to restore wholeness to the language experience and was developed for students with weak communications skills. While the major objective of the course is to improve written communications, listening, reading, and speaking activities are woven into the process in such a manner that each is developed and ultimately used to strengthen the student's written expression. Major course goals are:

1. Interrelating and permitting mutual reinforcement of reading, writing, speaking, and listening skills
2. Allowing students with complex skill deficiencies the additional

time and individualized attention required for them to approach proficiency
3. Acquainting students with major thinkers and contemporary intellectual issues as a content groundwork for success in other college courses

The course extends over two semesters, meets five days a week, and carries six hours of elective credit for all who complete it with a D or better average.

Early in the course, the instructor assesses the communications abilities of each student to determine strengths and weaknesses, using a combination of in-house and commercially prepared materials. Following the assessment, the instructor personalizes the learning experience, making it as compatible with the student's immediate learning goals and objectives as possible. For example, if a unit on the book report is stimulated by a requirement in another course, the unit will be personalized to meet the specific criteria established by the teacher of that course. Thus, if the student is to prepare a book report on *Animal Farm* for a history course, he or she would likely be advised to spend time exploring parallels with the Russian Revolution and its aftermath or the significance of the name *Napoleon*.

What the communications instructor attempts to do is help the student understand that scholars and writers approach the same phenomenon from the perspective of their own disciplines. If the student is to learn to cope effectively with the disciplines, she or he must understand the perspective of the discipline. The student learns that a book report is not just a report on a book, but a report from the perspective of a given discipline. The course does not pretend to equip the student with a sophisticated understanding of a given discipline, but it does try to provide a point of entry from which students can build disciplinary sophistication.

Whenever possible, students' interests and skill needs are prime determinants of their learning activities. The path to the achievement of specific learning objectives is determined jointly by the student and teacher. If a particular path is found less than satisfactory, other paths are explored. And in choosing a path, consideration is given not only to the student's weakness, but also to his or her strengths.

One of the rather unusual aspects of the course is the use of Benjamin Bloom's hierarchy of cognitive skills to assess learning needs.[9] Application of Bloom's taxonomy to actual student performance enables the instructor to determine students' strengths and weaknesses and to work toward balancing out the knowledge, intellectual abilities, and skills needed to help students achieve their particular goals.

Bloom's taxonomy is also useful as a means of structuring exercises that develop essay writing, test-taking, reading, and discussion skills. The following are examples of activities at each level of the taxonomy.

At the memory level
1. Accurate reproduction of information from lecture note outlines
2. Short answer definitions, identification
3. Simple reporting techniques (inverted pyramid)
4. Sample assignments
   a. Briefly define the term *multiversities*.
   b. Name the three blunders John I of England made with regard to the power of the monarchy.

At the translation level
1. Summary
2. Explanation of process
3. Conveying similar information through different forms for different purposes
4. Sample assignments
   a. Explain what is meant by a "two-headed Janus."
   b. Describe the communication process represented by the diagram $S\frac{M}{F}R$

At the interpretation level
1. Predicting patterns of development inherent in certain sets of information
2. Drawing conclusions
3. Deriving topic sentences
4. Comparing and contrasting
5. Cause and effect
6. Sample assignments
   a. Discuss the relationship between the concept of the ownership of land and the nature of power.
   b. Contrast Julian Huxley's hopes for the future with his predictions.

At the application level
1. Developing examples
2. Applying concepts and theories to your own experience
3. Locating and using supporting information
4. Sample assignments

    a. Explain why dysfunctional communication occurred in your group discussion.
    b. Assume that you have a young dog that chases cars. Describe how you would use Skinnerian theory to train the dog not to chase cars.

At the analysis level
1. Clarifying and categorizing information
2. Development and refutation of argument
3. Proofreading for inadequate and/or illogical transitions
4. Sample assignments
    a. Discuss why George Orwell might be said to have missed the mark in *1984*.
    b. Explore the idea that equality of opportunity is a contradiction in terms.

At the synthesis level
1. Deriving original thesis statements which can be supported
2. Formulating extended definitions
3. Sample assignments
    a. Forrester and others have shown that continuance of existing trends in the use of nonreplenishable resources, population growth, capital investment, and pollution does not make for a workable future. Design a possible future in which these factors are not in conflict.
    b. If we accept the statement to be true that large systems eventually break down, what, in terms of our society, would be the logical outcome of such breakdown, which particular systems would be affected, and why?

At the evaluation level
Deriving, developing, and applying criteria for judgment. Sample assignments:
    a. Under what circumstances can you justify Machiavellian theory and why?
    b. Discuss your use of the term *relevant*. What bases do you use for considering something to be "relevant" or "irrelevant" and why?

A separately numbered section of the course is reserved largely for students in two special programs: Special Services, the collegiate component of the federally supported TRIO programs, and Breakthrough, a program developed to increase the percentage of minority students attending a university located in a service region that is predominantly white. Students coming to the university through these two programs are often found to be weak in one or more basic skills areas.

Each Special Services or Breakthrough student is administered an in-house placement test to assess thinking skills as well as reading, writing, and study skills. Those who do well enter the standard freshman English courses offered by the English Department. Those with considerable weaknesses are placed in a special communications course, where more time and attention can be devoted to their particular needs and problems.

Because every effort is made to tailor the course to suit the students' interests, objectives, and learning styles, many teaching methods are employed. These include group work, tutoring, projects, lecture-discussion, role playing, and simulation gaming. Particular emphasis is placed upon the development of questioning techniques.

A variety of instructional materials and learning activities is also used, including articles, books, posters, and films. Organized thematically, these materials form the content core of the course. While important, the content is not simply an end in itself, but is also a means of improving the students' skills in such areas as oral and written reports, the short essay, use of contrast and comparison, development of the main idea, information retrieval, debating, logical thinking, and the like. The skills emphasized in the course are selected for their importance to future academic success. The course instructor regularly consults with faculty in each of the disciplines to verify the actual behaviors expected of students as well as to obtain ideas on modifications of the course content.

To evaluate performance, students are tested on their ability to use factual information in the building and testing of concepts derived from readings, films, and discussions. Students are evaluated informally on their ability to articulate sound concepts orally and in writing. Self-rating scales are also employed, and these self-ratings, along with other assessment information, are utilized in periodic conferences with the instructor. Evaluation is also based on class attendance, classroom behavior, degree of effort, and degree of improvement in diagnosed and self-selected problem areas.

Since the course is designed to be two semesters in length, an incomplete (I) is typically awarded at the end of the first semester. However, the instructor does discuss the student's general level of performance in a conference at the end of the initial grading period. At the end of the course, students may receive a letter grade which removes the I from their transcript. In certain cases, the student may carry the I grade into a third semester. If it is not removed, as specified in the negotiated contract with the instructor, the I automatically becomes an F. The grading system grew out of the belief that students learn and mature at different rates and is designed to remain nonpunitive for as long as possible.

We have briefly described basic writing programs at three types of institutions—a university, a technical institute, and a community college—that are members of the Western North Carolina Consortium.[10] These programs share common elements, but they also differ in substantial ways. The divergence is surely a strength, for it means that different approaches to the teaching of basic writing are being explored and implemented and that members of the consortium are seeking to adapt whatever approach they use to fit the special circumstances of their institution.

5 A Writing Laboratory Model

Patrick Hartwell
University of Cincinnati

> Hartwell deals with the writing laboratory facility, a component of most basic writing programs, although the name of such facilities may vary. The practical problems encountered and goals realized through this model are discussed, as are the pedagogical and theoretical implications.

"Well," the department head said, pushing the chair back from the desk and pausing for a moment, "nothing else seems to work; we might as well try a writing lab." And so we did. Robert H. Bentley and I were given preliminary responsibility for designing the laboratory at the University of Michigan-Flint. Since Bob has a finely honed systems analysis mind, we began by considering basic questions of structure and theory and derived our specific day-to-day procedures from those primary assumptions. Thus, I'll discuss our experiences in terms of those questions, moving from structure to assumptions to procedures, and then turn to consider the more general implications of this model for college-level basic education.

Structure of the Laboratory

The Writing Laboratory opened in the spring of 1971, taught by Bob Bentley. It was offered as English 199: The Writing Laboratory, awarding one to three credits (repeatable for a maximum of four credits) on a laboratory basis. Two hours of laboratory time being considered the equivalent of a normal classroom session, in our fourteen-week semesters students had to accumulate twenty-eight hours to earn one credit (an average of two hours per week), fifty-six hours to earn two credits, and so on. The laboratory was open daily from 10 a.m. to 3 p.m. for individual work, and an optional laboratory class was scheduled from 3 p.m. to 5 p.m. two days a week for group workshops. Occasionally, the laboratory was open evenings to accommodate night students. Credit earned counted for the degree, but it did not fulfill the freshman English requirement. Although it replaced a noncredit remedial course required of some students, the Writing Laboratory was in no way required, our enrollment coming entirely from faculty and counseling referrals and word of mouth. We logged student attendance on a form showing the hours the student had spent and the total hours accumulated, along with a staff member's notes on what the student had done and might be expected to do on his or her next visit. The logs were filed in individual folders, along with all the work the student did in the laboratory. The folders thus comprised a continuing record of student progress.

Credit-upon-performance and continuous enrollment were established with the help of the registrar and faculty committees. Full-time students could enroll in the course at essentially any time during the semester; they were enrolled for zero credits, with both credit and grade awarded at the end of the semester. Further, we made an oral commitment to students enrolled in the course that they would receive at least a C grade if they completed the necessary hours, feeling that if we hadn't been able to help a student who had spent from twenty-eight to eighty-four hours in the laboratory, the fault was ours rather than the student's. And, as it turned out, none of us working in the laboratory felt that we ever gave an unearned C—our failures were those who just didn't show up.

That first semester, Bob Bentley awarded credit to thirty-three students, who averaged about two credits each. I taught the laboratory course the next semester and awarded credit to fifty-five students. After that, the department was able to release two instructors to team-teach the course, a procedure which continued until 1975, when a full-time instructional associate was hired to coordinate the laboratory, and the department went back to assigning a single instructor to the course. In 1972 the faculty approved English 100, College Reading Skills, as a regular academic offering, and, though the Writing Laboratory was physically distinct from the Reading Laboratory, instructors began to think of the two as an entity, a combined reading/writing laboratory. A course titled "English 399: Advanced Writing Laboratory" was added to the catalog in 1974, to meet the needs of upper-division students who wanted to improve their writing skills for graduate and professional schools or for employment. English 199 now enrolls about 75 students a semester, and English 399 10 to 12; the laboratory also assists 150 to 200 students a semester on a drop-in basis, primarily to support the freshman English program.

This structure was designed to create a learning situation that (1) would not be stigmatized as a "bonehead" or "remedial" program; (2) would allow individual needs to be dealt with individually; (3) would not repeat the failure situations of the past, in high school and earlier; and, in fact, (4) would make failure impossible. These goals seemed basic structural prerequisites as Bob and I talked over the developmental program with our colleagues. We had, as a department, been increasingly dissatisfied with the rigidity of the standard Berkeley Subject A model of noncredit "bonehead English," and we designed a structure that gave us much more flexibility. Individual students, depending on their skills and motivations, might be advised to take English 100 before taking the first-semester freshman English course, English 101, and they might also be advised to take English 199 concurrently with 101. Other students might combine English 100 and 101, using the Writing Laboratory on a drop-in basis. Still others, with adequate reading skills but writing deficiencies, might take English 199 for two or even three credits, either concurrently with or prior to English 101.

Bob and I started with a clear sense of the place of a developmental English program within the university and the department. We felt that developmental English ought to give college credit, and real credit, within an academic department, and later studies have shown the wisdom of that assumption.[1] We also felt that developmental English ought to be a commitment of the department as a whole, not something that was given to a junior, often untenured, faculty member to bear alone. After agreeing on a team-taught laboratory, the department was able to involve many faculty volunteers, usually teaming an experienced laboratory instructor with an inexperienced one. Each new instructor contributed his or her own emphases to the laboratory, and all of us who worked in the laboratory felt that the close exposure to the writing process improved our perceptions of student writing and student learning, and thereby improved our own teaching, both in composition courses and in general. At one point, about half of the members of the department had had laboratory experience, and most of us felt that this commitment improved the quality of our developmental and freshman programs.[2] Priorities shifted as the department grew, however, and the initial goal of full department involvement was not achieved.

Assumptions

We began the planning and implementation of the Writing Laboratory with clear-cut assumptions about the transmission of literacy. Bob and I were both aware of the hundred years of research showing that instruction in rote grammar was at best useless and at worst harmful.[3] We also knew, as linguists, that our students were verbally and logically competent adults.[4] Thus, we defined our task as teaching a certain kind of *performance*—writing performance, a tacit, knowing-how skill—rather than effecting linguistic or cognitive competence by teaching conscious mastery of formal "rules" of language or logic. One implication of this assumption was that we took a different view of the dialects that our students came to us with, dialects of black or Chicano speakers, or Appalachian or rural dialects, all perceived as socially nonstandard in Flint, Michigan. These dialects were not for us impediments to mastering literacy, but primary strengths, for they not only shared the basic meaning patterns of all English dialects, but also had been exercised in complex rhetorical contexts.[5]

Such an assumption led us to place major stress on the communicative aspect of writing, on situational context, voice, audience, and paradigmatic form. In a real sense, then, we inverted the nineteenth-century hierarchy of *skills* which regarded "correctness" in pronunciation as a prerequisite to correctness in writing and correctness in surface detail—grammar and spelling—as a prerequisite to larger elements of form. We replaced it with a quite different hierarchy, one that was broadly cognitive, stressing process and purpose rather than structure and correctness, the larger potentialities of style and form rather than grammar and usage. Since our goal was full adult literacy, we wanted to place no artificial, school-determined learning blocks in front of that goal. Students who wanted to become literate adults, we felt, should start acting like literate adults, not be sidetracked into mechanical exercises that had no immediate application to functional literacy.

Similarly, we felt that the connection between speech and writing occurred at the highest level, the level of communication, rather than at the low level of surface features of dialect and written codes. Thus, we viewed reading and writing as complexly interrelated, and we felt that it was mastery of this abstract code of literacy that affected speech, rather than the other way around. Finally, from what we knew about the attitudes of nontraditional students, we formulated another primary assumption, "attitude change precedes performance change"—that is, the nontraditional student must be given confidence in his or her ability to perform a task before the task will be performed successfully.

At that time, we were conscious of being influenced by available theories of composition,[6] but we were also in part just guessing, motivated by simple dissatisfaction with the models available to us. Since 1971, researchers have given us greater confidence in our initial assumptions, for a number of studies have stressed the importance of tacit cognitive models in learning. Chomsky, for example, has established a causal relationship between amount and variety of reading and mastery of syntax, and Brause has extended that finding to identify a nine-stage developmental ability to process semantic ambiguity which may well reflect gradual mastery of the print code rather than direct instruction.[7] Both reading theorists and linguists have become more aware of the importance of mastering codes rather than being told about them, and rhetoricians and students of the composing process are increasingly aware of the centrality of rhetorical context and the importance of stylistic choice.[8] Such studies support our initial hunch that internal models are best changed by activities rather than by memorizing rules and injunctions, by doing rather than learning about.

Laboratory Procedures

Our most important procedural decision was to use an undergraduate staff for individual tutoring of students enrolled in the laboratory. The student staff was chosen to be ethnically and sexually representative of the students they worked with, and we tended to look for people who were sensitive to the needs of others rather than simply English majors. In time, many of our staff were students who had themselves earned credit in the Writing Laboratory. The student staff—originally five, now eight to twelve—was paid on an hourly basis, either through department funds or through work-study. They were asked to take a nine-credit-hour training program: an introductory course in linguistics; an upper-division composition course, Rhetoric and the Writing Process; and a three-credit-hour course of directed readings in urban education. The directed readings allowed us to share studies of the nontraditional student,[9] and it also allowed us to schedule regular staff meetings.

Staff meetings were held in the evening at a faculty member's home—once a week at the beginning of a semester, every second or third week later. It was common for faculty not released for laboratory instruction to attend the meetings, which combined a social gathering with a broad-ranging discussion of urban education and a careful look at the progress of students enrolled in the laboratory. This last process—"going through the files"—gave us, as a staff, a shared sense of the progress and needs of individual students and a direction and specific assignments for them. We spent a good bit of time diagnosing student writing at the beginning of a year, making the student staff aware of the need to "read between the lines" of the work of basic writers, to ignore individual surface errors, and to seek out implicit structures and needs. The staff's background in linguistics and rhetoric proved invaluable in such analyses: they learned to respond to error patterns rather than to errors as such and to develop a rhetorical vocabulary for talking about writing. Later discussions dealt more broadly with institutional, social, and racial factors in the transmission of literacy.

Our student staff was primarily responsible for achieving our basic goals. They broke down the artificialities of the student-teacher relationship and of the conventional classroom—and more than that, they brought an immediate sense of the students' interaction with the university that we as faculty could not share. We found ourselves learning as much from the intuitions and analyses of our student staff as they learned from us.[10]

Inevitably, the atmosphere of the Writing Laboratory was loose and informal, occasionally plain noisy. Writing samples just completed were often read to others working in the laboratory; questions would be shouted out and problems shared; there was a constant sense of writing as an activity and a mode of communication. We had insisted that confidence-building be a primary goal, and it was a general rule that no negative comments were made about a piece of writing to the student, at least for the first part of his or her time in the laboratory. Weak writing was not the product of lazy, slovenly, or unthinking students; it reflected an inadequate mastery of aspects of the print code, aspects which could be isolated and learned.

The Instructional Protocol

When a student first came to the laboratory, we asked for an initial writing sample, often written with a staff member offering encouragement. In many cases our students showed a basic inability to put words on paper, a lack of scribal fluency. Speed writing five- or ten-minute timed writings, ideally written with a staff member or instructor writing alongside, worked well with such students. We found that a few days of practice always increased the number of words written per minute, and that crude measure gave many students their first visible success in writing. We found speed writing also useful for students whose writing was marked by bloated diction and empty structural elaboration —Macrorie's "Engfish" or Zoellner's "schizokinetic scribophobia." The mere physical pressure to put words on paper didn't allow such students time to think up fancy words or elaborate sentences.

Other basic writing students succeeded much too well at speed writing (their reading scores often showed that they read at a high rate of speed, 500 to 600 words per minute, but with minimal comprehension).[11]

Talking with such students, we learned that they survived in other courses by memorizing sentences from textbooks, with little conceptual grasp of what those sentences meant.[12] We also found that their writing repertoire was limited to one or two canned papers. With these students, we found it important to talk out their perceptions about reading and writing and to contrast them with those of successful students working as staff members. We found the tape recorder an invaluable tool for such students—the process of talking out ideas to a listener could be transferred back to the more abstract process of communicating in speech.

The tape recorder, in fact, proved successful at all stages of the writing process.[13] The drop-in student who had no ideas for a freshman theme assignment usually found that he or she did indeed have ideas after a few minutes of taped talk with a staff member. Students were encouraged to read first drafts into the tape recorder and then listen to them played back. They could then often identify weaknesses in sentence structure, coherence, and development. We also found that students who tended to leave off -s and -ed endings in writing tended to insert them in their speech, when faced with the somewhat formal situation of speaking into a recorder. Thus, they could move back from their tacit awareness of grammatical signals in speech to the forms used to code those signals in writing. Most of the errors in -ed endings occurred when the written -ed was realized as a spoken /t/, as in *walked*, and this fact supported our feeling that basic writing students had simply not mastered certain print coding features. In this case, we found it useful to connect the written -ed with its four spoken realizations—/d/ as in *defined*, /əd/ as in *rounded*, /t/ as in *talked*, and the null realization /∅/—in many contexts in all dialects. With this connection made, we could begin to improve surface correctness without explicitly raising such grammatical concepts as past tense or regular and irregular verbs.

Once a student had mastered scribal fluency and had gained confidence in his or her abilities, we turned often in one of two directions: a transfer of the student's well-defined sense of voice and rhetorical stance to its embodiment in the print code or a stress on writing as choice and manipulation. "Voice" in speaking was pinned down in print in a number of activities, both individual and group, most involving a game or play situation that built upon developing scribal fluency, such as identifying the qualities conveyed by the voice and style of a taped speaker and then imitating that speaker; adopting a specific voice for a particular purpose (a professor cancelling class, a driver talking a police officer out of a ticket); and identifying a parody of a style or writing parodies. Sentence manipulation always involved reworking existing texts in order to minimize rhetorical invention and focus on the possibilities of syntactic choice. Sentence combining and even classical imitation were used. Bob Bentley in particular was able to see the importance of journalism as an initial form for writing, giving students the basic form of a newspaper report and the new information from which a report was to be constructed.[14]

Journalism allowed us to move from scribal fluency, rhetorical context, and style to the concept of form. The form of a newspaper report has three advantages: it forces students to make decisions about main and supporting ideas and thereby enforces a skill basic to both reading and writing;[15] its strategy of form directly parallels the strategy of an essay examination and thus teaches a basic study skill; and it enforces the need for careful predication of statements—not that something was true, but that somebody asserted that something was true.

At this point—in an idealized overview of student progress—we tended to move from the closed form of journalism to the idea of open form, of how discourse is elaborated in response to idea and audience. Many staff members used Christensen paragraph analysis or Gorrell's concept of commitment and response to increase the texture and coherence of ideas in students' writing.[16] Others worked with the reading-writing process by assigning challenging essays and following up with summaries and critical responses. In the laboratory class we experimented with chain paragraphs (each person in a group adding a sentence to a paragraph while attempting to maintain coherence), with scrambled paragraphs, and with predicting the movement of professional writers sentence by sentence.[17] Such activities and analyses inevitably moved from questions of form to larger questions of strategy and argument.

Study skills, usage, and surface detail in grammar and spelling received a secondary priority in the laboratory, for we found that many students mastered them indirectly, as their higher-level skills in reading and writing improved. We did offer regular workshops in note-taking and test-taking, open to all students, and found them very popular. We would occasionally provide mock lectures with mock exams, stressing the need to subordinate rote detail to larger understanding. And we often learned that student staff members who were enrolled in other courses with laboratory students had set up informal study groups to review notes and prepare for exams.

We tried to stress the full potential of actual writing, treating surface detail as a code and game. Instead of rules of punctuation, we stressed the practice of professionals, guessing at their punctuation until students controlled semicolons, colons, and dashes as well as commas.[18] We taught the fragment by examining its use in advertising and informal writing. We taught *-s* and *-ed* endings by exploring their disappearance in public use. And we taught vocabulary by exploring how roots are expanded (from *fess* to *confess* and *profess*, *profess* to *professor*, *profession*, *professionally*, *unprofessorial*, and so on).

Of course, students came to us with other needs and were treated differently. Some came motivated only to learn grammar and spelling, and we taught them both, often suggesting that they broaden their writing activities as they continued in the laboratory. Spelling was easy enough to teach with available programmed texts or tapes and workbooks—as long as the "spelling problem" was not a symptom of an underlying reading deficiency.[19] Grammar was a different matter, since none of the available texts seemed as effective as individual work with the student's own writing.[20] Others came to us with writing needs that we felt were only symptoms of psychological uncertainties, and we worked closely with the counseling office with such students.

We were pleased, as the laboratory developed, to see an increasing number of students whose needs went beyond basic skills. Many older students returning to school, uncertain about their study skills and uneasy in the university environment, used the laboratory as a confidence-builder, reviewing the skills of taking notes, reading texts, preparing for and taking examinations. The study skills tests in the McGraw-Hill Basic Skills System were a good starting point for such students, though more as a way of demonstrating that they did indeed have college-level skills than as a diagnostic test. And we were quite frankly surprised by the number of juniors and seniors, mostly in pre-law and the social sciences, who came to the laboratory to prepare themselves for graduate school. Our first upper-division students simply dropped in on their own, but gradually the social science faculty began recommending the laboratory to their students. We developed a rigorous set of précis-writing exercises for these students, training some of our staff to edit deadwood and letting students compare their précis with the abstract written by the author. We sent these students to professional journals, to report on the form and style of communication in their field. We often devised special exercises in analysis, asking students to isolate assumptions and to identify schools of opinion. One such exercise provided a number of definitions of language, culled from traditional, structuralist, and generative grammars, and guided students to a formulation of the assumptions of the different schools. Such a mixture of students soon removed any lingering sense of the laboratory as the home of "bonehead English."

Evaluation and Validity of the Model

All of us involved in the laboratory felt that the procedures were successful and that our laboratory had validated an approach to developmental education that differed from most models available when we began. We were not able, however, to obtain funding for a full-scale evaluation of the Writing Laboratory. Standardized pretests and posttests (the Houghton Mifflin *College English Placement Test*) showed significant improvement, even though the assumptions of the test were not those of the laboratory. Greg Waters was able to make a more interesting evaluation in 1976, comparing the success of a sample of Writing Laboratory students in other classes with a random sample of university students in general; it showed that the laboratory students, on the whole, did slightly better than the sample of other students.

Such informal evidence does not prove the validity of our initial assumptions or their implications, and this summary treatment inevitably ignores our successes and failures with individual students. It does suggest, however, that the dominant model of developmental education —teaching students grammar in required, noncredit courses—may no longer be the only model to consider.

Of course, the precise model outlined here cannot be directly transferred to other institutions. Two-year colleges are less likely to have tutors available and are unable to use them, as we did, for two or three years. Many four-year colleges, with a better source of tutors, may lack the support courses for staff training. But aspects of our model have been adopted at other schools, especially the structural features of laboratory credit, credit upon performance, and continuing files. Yet, visitors to the Flint Laboratory and audiences at professional meetings have been most uncertain about those aspects that we felt most positively about—the use of peer tutors and the hierarchy of goals. Therefore, I have been particularly interested in the adaptation of the model made by Diane Menendez at the University of Cincinnati. She has supplemented the laboratory with small-group classes meeting once a week—a necessity on a large and impersonal campus—and is working to establish the laboratory as a resource for the freshman English program, in addition to providing developmental instruction as such, and as a center for training graduate and undergraduate students in the teaching of basic writing.

General Implications of the Laboratory Model

There is, finally, a more important point than adaptability to be made about this model, one relevant to the teaching of college composition in general. Our models of developmental education follow expectations of college students and our paradigms for tea[c]... writing. The paradigm we have inherited from the nineteen[th]... which stresses grammar, usage, and the fixed methods of d... isolates the classroom from the larger activity of commu[nication]... limits the inventive capabilities of our students to the mecha... manipulation of the socially correct and intellectually obvious. At worst, as Ohmann has argued, we prepare, through this model, capitalist bureaucrats trained not to ask questions.[21] McDermott has noted that, as a result, we have established success and failure in learning to read and write on a social class basis:

> Each year, more and more are sorted out until the "select few" reach college. The word "select" should not be taken in its elitist sense. By the time they enter college, some people may be more select because their enculturation to school equips them to do college work. We should not make the mistake, however, of thinking that the select few were selected for any reason other than that they were most like their teachers.[22]

McDermott's analysis of school failure is a valid picture of elementary and secondary education. But we in colleges no longer see only the "select few"; we see minds with legitimate goals from a cross section of society. The answer to the crisis in basics is not to return to the basics, for the existing paradigm explains the very failure we struggle with and against. The answer is to develop new paradigms for literacy and for learning. Such new paradigms will profoundly change developmental education. They should also profoundly change our sense of the profession of English and the training of students who wish to enter it.

6 The Rhetoric Program at Boston University's College of Basic Studies

Harry Crosby
Boston University

Crosby presents an interdisciplinary approach to writing instruction presently working very effectively at Boston University. This approach is based on the convictions that teaching basic writing is not solely the right or responsibility of an English department and that it can be pursued with great success through a united effort by several disciplines.

Very few writing programs are as accountability minded as the Rhetoric Department of Boston University's College of Basic Studies. One evidence of this concern for accountability is the annual Writing Gain Study. The rhetoric faculty looks out with some surprise at an academic world which questions whether instruction can be evaluated and writing progress measured. Our Gain Study is eloquent testimony that both are possible.

In September each entering freshman writes an impromptu theme on one of four topics. By tinkering with the phrasing and rejecting topics too hard or too easy, we now have four topics which yield approximately the same grade distribution:

> Will the electronic media (television, telephone, computers) replace writing?
> Are Americans making a new religion of sports?
> Are today's films merely entertainment, or are they something more, like art or education?
> What is the future of travel?

The September papers are filed away, and in December, May, or both, each student writes another impromptu paper on another of the subjects. In May the September and/or December themes are shuffled with the later papers and scored on a standarized Theme Analysis Blank (see Figure 1). The rhetoric faculty do not know the date of the paper, the student's name, or the student's teacher; thus, the grading is triple

Boston University
College of Basic Studies

Theme Analysis Blank
Division of Rhetoric

Purpose	0 1 2 3 4
Title	
Introduction	
appeal	
orientation	
significance	
purpose/thesis indication	
Conclusion	
summary	
echo of introduction	
Structure	0 1 2 3 4
Pattern of organization: narration; description; definition; analysis; comparison/contrast; classification; cause/effect; judgment	
Paragraphs	
sequence	
topic sentences	
appropriateness	
Transitions	
clarity	
appropriateness	
Substance	0 1 2 3 4
Relevant	
Accurate	
Sufficient	
Authoritative	
Style	0 1 2 3 4
Clear, efficient, appropriate	
Diction: accurate, balanced, concise	
Sentences: varied (construction, length, complexity)	
structured (apt, ordered)	
fluent	
Tone: consistent; suitable for author, message, audience	
Voice	
Conventions	0 1 2 3 4
neatness, legibility, margins, pagination, proofreading, title placement, punctuality, endorsement, suitability of paper (size, weight, texture, no ripped edges)	
Mechanics	-1 -2 -3 -4 -5 -6 -7 -8
comma splice, agreement of pronouns/verbs, illogical fragments, dangling modifiers, run-on sentences, spelling, punctuation, other grammatical conventions	
	TOTAL _____

Underlining of the above by instructor indicates deficiency; circling indicates excellence.

Fig. 1. Standardized scoring blank used for rating papers by Rhetoric Department faculty at Boston University.

blind. Since each batch has approximately one-fourth of the papers on each topic, there is no way to tell an early paper from a later one; any paper that makes an allusion to a fall sport, a current event, or a college teacher is ignored in computations. Since the rhetoric faculty uses the Theme Analysis Blank habitually and has had frequent rating practice sessions, reliability at worst is around .750 and usually around .900.

For six years we have seen an average student gain of four points on a rating scale with a possible score of 20. On our scale this gain is enough to move students up one letter grade. However, more sophisticated analysis of this progress is necessitated by the ceiling effect of the grading scale—that is, if a student gets a 17 in September, he or she has a small chance, mathematically, of making significant improvement. This kind of analysis shows that in large measure September F writers became C minus writers, C writers become B writers, and C plus and B minus move up into the B plus and A minus range.

The accompanying quartile analysis chart (Figure 2) shows how our students fared in September, December, and May, 1977-78. The vertical representation at the left of the chart describes the entire freshman class; it shows that the poorest September paper received a mark of minus 3, an F, and the highest received a mark of 18, B plus. The

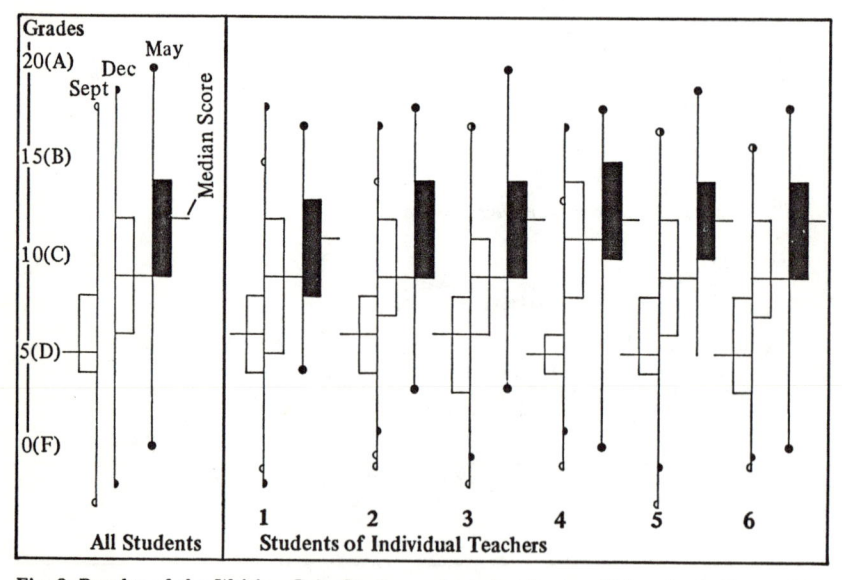

Fig. 2. Results of the Writing Gain Study conducted at Boston University in September, December, and May, 1977-78. The verticals at the far left show results for the entire freshman class. The boxed areas on each vertical represent the middle 50 percent of each class.

median score was 5, a D. The 25th percentile score, one-fourth from the bottom, was 4 and the 75th, 7. Thus, the chart shows that the middle 50 percent of the class moved from a range of 4-7 in September to a range of 6-12 in December and to a range of 9-14 in May. The median score of 5 in September moved up to a 9 in December and a 12 in May, or from a D to a C minus and on to a C plus.

The Gain Study and a number of other studies we have made provide the basis for our confidence in the writing program we offer our students. It is my purpose now to describe that program.

The College of Basic Studies

The rhetoric program at Boston University can best be understood if examined as part of what has been called "a successful human reclamation project." That project, now twenty-five years old, is the College of Basic Studies (CBS). Each year CBS admits approximately 600 students. Whereas the rest of Boston University prefers its applicants to be in the top third of their high school class and comfortably over 600 on their college boards, the College of Basic Studies admits students who are in the bottom third of their class and whose board scores are as low as 300. These students are called "referrals." They are admitted to CBS because other parts of Boston University rejected them.

Two years later many CBS students transfer to other Boston University colleges, and as juniors and seniors come up with grade points that equal or surpass those of their new peers. Some of the academically most successful, heady with their newly developed academic prowess, apply for transfer outside of BU. They have been accepted by and graduated from almost every kind of college and university.

Besides the CBS student who is a referral, there is a second kind of student, the direct applicant, who comes because of the school's unique reputation. Many high school advisors, knowing of a very poor graduate who did well at CBS, believe that an average student (or better) could have an even greater development. They reason that a school having such success with late bloomers could do just as well with the almost fully flowered, and they have been right. CBS has helped many good students become academically excellent.

History of the CBS

In the late 1940s a group of young faculty wanted to remedy what they considered a scandal in higher education. They felt that university freshmen and sophomores, usually taught by graduate assistants, should have full-time, experienced, committed teachers. Secondly, protesting the extreme compartmentalization of the university, they wished to develop a general education curriculum.

Fortunately for the reformers, a class of students arrived who were causing guilt feelings among prestigious Northeastern universities. Fresh from World War II, veterans knocked at the doors of such institutions. The well-prepared ones were received hospitably, but the less well prepared were shunted off to institutions with less demanding admissions standards. Thus, to solve several problems at once, officials at Boston University approved an interdisciplinary lower division program on the understanding that it would be primarily for the unprepared student. As a result Boston University's College of Basic Studies was born.

For the next decade the Junior College (as CBS was then called) existed under a basket. Many of the Boston University faculty were uneasy about the Junior College, whose admission standards brought down the total university average to the point where Boston University could not claim to have the high admissions standards desired for the competition with other New England institutions.

In the early 60s, however, there was a change. When the president of Boston University was invited to bring with him his outstanding senior to a White House conference on higher education, the president learned to his astonishment that the senior adjudged so impressive had been a student at the Junior College. Urged on by this circumstance, the university did an intensive follow-up study that revealed Junior College products did very well indeed as juniors and seniors in other university programs. In all but two of the other colleges, CBS students actually had higher averages than the students who originally had adequate entrance requirements. Since then the successes of CBS students at Boston University and elsewhere have become a proud tradition of Boston University.

Basic to CBS and its rhetoric program are two intrinsic qualities: the team system and the interdisciplinary curriculum. Every student who attends the College of Basic Studies is assigned to a team of five professors, one each from the Department of Humanities, Social Science, Science, Psychology and Counseling, and Rhetoric. All teachers on the team but the counselor have private offices off the same common room. Since this anteroom has students' mailboxes, tables, chairs, and usually a bubbling coffeepot, the team suite serves as a central headquarters for the 100 to 120 students assigned to a team and makes it easy indeed for them to have quick and personal contact with their faculty. Once each week, the team of instructors meets to confer about syllabuses, interdisciplinary assignments, and successes and failures with individual students. Each student is thus a member of a small college within a college within a large university.

A second feature of the College of Basic Studies is that for its entire history it has been struggling to develop a defensible program of general education, by answering two questions: (1) What commonality of skills, content, and attitude do we expect of a student who is supposed to have a college education? and (2) What is the best way to teach students those qualities?

The interdisciplinary nature of the CBS program is aided by the team system, but it is established by the syllabus of each course. The Science Department teaches a year each of natural and biological science, with attention not only to biology, physics, chemistry, geology, zoology, and meteorology, but also to the history of the science and the development of the scientific method. The Social Science program includes history, economics, political science, and sociology, with special attention to how social scientists think and what data they use. The Division of Humanities teaches poetry, fiction, drama, film, and philosophy. Attention is given to the development and function of the artist. As an example of the interdisciplinary approach, combined attention can be given to the rite of passage because at the same moment the Science Department is studying biological change, the Psychology Department is studying adolescent development, the Social Science Department is studying ceremonies of primitive societies, and the Humanities Department is reading "Of This Time, Of That Place" and other stories about the young. It is customary for instructors from various disciplines to share classroom activities, but a primary catalyst for interdisciplinary activity is the rhetoric paper.

The Rhetoric Program

The rhetoric faculty consists of two full professors, two associate professors, two assistant professors, and one instructor. Although some of the faculty occasionally teach literature in the summer or in the evenings, the entire faculty is committed professionally to the teaching of freshman English. All of the faculty have had a good deal of prior experience in the teaching of written composition, and most have made numerous contributions to the professional literature.

The rhetoric faculty has the primary objective of helping its students learn to communicate significant thoughts and information effectively. Since the students' first and most urgent need for these skills is to express what they have learned in their other courses, the rhetoric staff is pleased to take advantage of this motivation and willingly assumes the role of a service department; whenever possible, assignments are keyed to the study and writing needs of other departments.

To achieve our objectives, the rhetoric staff knows no better method than to demand that our students read, write, listen, and speak frequently under close supervision. Each freshman is required to write approximately 7,000 words per year, usually in the form of seven themes or extended exercises per semester for the rhetoric course; in addition, the other courses require at least one paper per semester that usually involves the rhetoric teacher in critique and grading.

Confronted with a wide range of referral and direct applicant students, most of them quickly bored and many of them with low motivation and short attention spans, the faculty has had to come up with an approach which is applicable to all and is characterized by immediate success. Our approach is based on our perception that nearly every decade has required a deeper explanation of why students have difficulty writing. Thirty years ago students had to remove grammatical barbarisms and improve their writing style to be better writers. For that reason the use of the handbook of grammar, spelling, and punctuation was the legitimate approach. A decade later, students, with their decreased reading experience and skill, also had to have models which showed how to unify (e.g., "write with a purpose" or have "the argumentative edge") and structure a paragraph. In addition to basic grammar, they had to learn what development was and why one word was better than another, i.e., where it lay on the ladder of abstraction. In the last five years, students have done so little writing, often as few as 350 words in their senior year of high school, that they need to go back to the very beginning. They need to know that a composition has an introduction, a body, and a conclusion—and what happens in each one. Most importantly, they need to know how writers analyze their topic and structure their message—in short, how they think.

At the beginning our students need to be shown the many ways their manuscripts communicate. They need to know that a sloppy paper, with uneven margins, with the edge of the paper ripped into a messy lace work, with no title, with no page numbers, says very loudly indeed, "I do not care whether I have your attention and respect." They need to know that such a paper makes communication unlikely, if not impossible.

As a result, leaning on the psychologist's idea of positive reinforcement, we let our students know that we attach so much importance to legibility, conventions, and neatness that we will give them no less than a D on a paper if it fulfills the basic conventions and nothing more. During the first unit students are told that the use of a traditional-conventional pattern is so valuable that if they produce a work with a clear introduction, body, and a conclusion, they are on the way up the grade ladder to a C.

As years have passed, the rhetoric faculty has become less insistent upon demanding a thesis statement in the penultimate sentence of the introduction, because a thesis statement clearly expressed in an early draft seems to inhibit extensive and meaningful revision. If students decide early on exactly what they wish to say, they miss the valuable lesson that writing is discovery. When they have a thesis statement, they try to make their data fit; when they know what they are saying, they think their audience also knows, and they tend not to provide enough information, relying instead on generalizations and opinions. Therefore, early in the semester we emphasize the controlling question as purpose indicator. Students who prase a question at the end of their introduction have provided themselves with a test of what information is relevant and necessary. As they complete their paper, all they need ask is, "Am I answering my question?"

Most of our students get a form of C grade for their first two papers because early standards are clear and limited. Anyone can turn in a conventional, neat, legible paper; anyone can write a five-paragraph paper if he or she knows what is supposed to happen in each paragraph. An assignment that asks, for instance, why students are believed to be apathetic or why they think their high school did a good or poor job in making them feel prepared for college prompts them to have three paragraphs in the body of the paper, each beginning with the next point, i.e., a topic sentence. Other early assignments we have used include "three myths about young people today," "three surprises," and "three qualities of urban university students as noted in three weeks of school."

Prior to their third paper, students are told some new facts of life. They learn that just as they can earn positive points, they can lose them as inevitably if they do not follow certain grammatical and orthographic conventions. They are taught, if they do not already know, that when the World complains that Johnny and Johnnie can't write, what the World means is that they can't spell or punctuate or avoid grammatical troubles.

Our students are now introduced to the bottom part of our Theme Analysis Blank (see Figure 1) which indicates how they lose points. If they commit what we, speaking for the World, label a "glaring error" (illogical fragment, run-on sentence, comma splice, disagreement of verb and subject, faulty reference in a pronoun, misplaced or dangling modifier), they lose a half point. For a less offensive error in grammar, spelling, or punctuation, they lose a quarter point.

Aware of the real world of critical readers, our students are next led through a series of units which guarantee exposure to the patterns of thought we think they will need for analysis, exposition, and argumentation, in short, the writing they will do for the rest of their college careers and the rest of their lives.

The first unit is on basic structures: introduction with establishment of purpose, body, conclusion, and generative (topic) sentence, plus development in paragraphs. In the second unit we work on narration and description, to remind them of the need for the flow of an idea. During narration we point out the importance of verbs and adverbs; during description we stress what kind of nouns and adjectives communicate best. A sample writing assignment during this unit is a theme on the subject of "This Is My Home Town." With E.B. White's "Here Is New York" as their substantive model, students are asked to make a statement about their home town which they defend by describing the town or city and relating a series of narratives which justify the statement they have made in their introduction. In the rough draft, which they must submit, they are required to underline the nouns and adjectives in the description and the verbs and adverbs in the narrative. For their final draft they are asked to try to make their diction more vivid and specific.

In the third unit, students study the basic parts of an extended definition (classification, differentia, comparison and contrast, entymology, demonstration by illustration, contrast to synonyms) and its uses in various disciplines. They learn new uses of the dictionary. In this unit rhetoric teachers depend heavily upon the other departments, getting from them terms for writing assignments, such as *empiricism, transcendentalism, existentialism, triage, democracy,* and *capitalism.*

During unit four, on process analysis, students are taught not only how to use the patterns, but also to be more aware of the audience because a process assumes that the reader out there is going to have a behavior change. Whereas narration and description had patterns but not necessarily parts, students now seek a basis for interrupting process and breaking it into useful and meaningful steps. Here again rhetoric teachers rely on other departments for the subject matter, with one favorite topic being the steps of the scientific method. The last two units of the first semester take up classification and comparison-contrast, completing the patterns particularly needed for exposition, or the kind of communication necessary to get a reader to say "I understand."

In the second semester attention is turned to argumentation. Students learn the difference between the evidence used in argument for conviction and argument for action, i.e., what is needed to cause a reader to say "I agree" and "I will do what you ask." They learn to work with the patterns of cause and effect, judgment, stock issues, and problem and solution. In the middle of the semester, students do a research paper and learn to work with primary and secondary sources and advanced manuscript conventions.

We complete the year with the "content" of our course, a unit on the history and nature of language and one on epistemology and logic. The two units are something beyond a collection of facts. In our language study we try to help students develop a sense of how language changes. Their sense can be demonstrated, for instance, by a paper on the future of language, in which the student makes up a word and shows what lexicographical and etymological principles are demonstrated in its coinage. In the unit on epistemology and logic, for instance, we try to have students analyze the source and legitimacy of ideas currently being bandied about in the modern political and intellectual world.

Teaching of Style, Grammar, Spelling, and Punctuation

We have no scheduled units for style or mechanics. We do, however, attach great importance to them. Our Theme Analysis Blank (Figure 1) focuses student attention on the lesson that they can work very hard for two weeks on a paper and then ruin their grade by a careless last-minute proofreading. This arbitrarily tough policy almost invariably eliminates 85 percent of the grammar, spelling, and punctuation troubles. When errors are caused no longer by carelessness but by ignorance, we go to work with work sheets demonstrating errors made in current student papers. Each time we have a session on grammar, spelling, and punctuation, we stick to just one "error" and have students demonstrate they can consciously make the error and correct it.

We teach style the same way: diagnostically focused and paced. Our standards may not be high; we admit that we rarely help a student develop a really glossy style. Our goals are clarity, effectiveness, and appropriateness. We teach the ladder of abstraction to show why a specific word is better than a general one; we teach dictionary usage to help students find the exact word, perhaps even the metaphoric or figurative phrase; and we teach the difference between the loose and periodic sentence. Most of us also teach sentence imbedding, and to help students write with some grace, we do analyze the good style of our models.

Sample Assignments

Writing assignments of the Rhetoric Department should pass two tests: they should induce students to use the pattern currently being studied and, if possible, cause them to review a pattern previously studied. For instance, when we ask students to write a paper on the rite of passage, we stipulate that they are to define the term; describe specific rites of passage referred to in Margaret Mead's *Coming of Age in Samoa* or *Sex and Temperament*; and compare and/or contrast the rites in primitive societies discussed by Mead and encountered in the film *Walkabout* and "Agostino" and "The Story of My Dovecot." In addition students are required to write a narrative of an event in their own life which finally made them realize what a rite of passage is. Sample theses students developed during this assignment, which is read by the student's entire faculty, include "It was not until I came to college that I realized that what I had experienced at the age of fourteen was a rite of passage" and "I realize now that earlier societies have more definite rites of passage than in my time—and I am so much the poorer."

In another assignment the humanities and social science teachers ask students to explain what the book *Alive* demonstrates about the lessons of sociology, while the rhetoric teacher requires that their papers contain a narrative précis of what happened to the airliner passengers who crashed and survived in the Andes. Students are expected to define relevant sociology terms like *survival of the fittest, societal structure, division of labor,* and *values*. They are required to turn in rough drafts to show that they have revised their introduction and conclusion to make sure they have discussed what adds up to a central message. A sample thesis deduced by students was "In the short time the airliner passengers lived together, they synopsized the entire general history of civilization."

Another typical CBS writing assignment involved a science teacher who wished to check on how his students had mastered the scientific method. He passed out an account of how a mythical firm, the Pontecaro Orange Growers, tried to increase its sales by conducting and publicizing a research program which "proved" that drinking orange juice prevents colds. The rhetoric teacher, who at the time was working on research and manuscript techniques, was pleased at an opportunity to work in more practice on narration, description, process analysis, judgment, and problem-solution. The two professors, therefore, assigned a research paper in which students were to criticize the orange growers' research and suggest a more conclusive study.

The Theme Analysis Blank

Although we may not use it on every assignment, the Theme Analysis Blank (TAB) encourages teachers to indicate to student writers how they have mastered lessons being studied. Teacher time is saved by telling students that underlining indicates a deficiency but a circle around a comment indicates a strength. At least once a year, we have departmental meetings and ratings to standardize our grading.

The total of the numerical ratings of the TAB converts into letter grades according to the following scale: 19-20, A; 18, A-; 17, B+; 14-16, B; 13, B-; 12, C+; 9-11, C; 8, C-; 7, D+; 4-6, D; below 4, F.

Because of the potential negative points for grammar, spelling, and mechanics, there are many F's. Our department aims for this spread of semester grades: A, 10 percent; B, 20 percent; C, 40 percent; D, 20 percent; and F, 10 percent. However, in part because of the central tendency caused by so many grades, the curve bulges at the center and we usually end up with 5 percent at the two ends. We do try to discriminate; at the end of the first semester, because of low grades, about 5 percent of the class is dismissed from the school. About one-third of the dismissed petition for readmission and repeat the first semester.

Problems

Although we are generally pleased with our course, we still have problems. The first difficulty is that, in the main, we seem not to have a truly stimulating course. We are probably too pedestrian and unimaginative. Each year our students complete a detailed questionnaire, and each year they comment too often that the course is "dull" and "boring." Our students are nice: they tell us they like us, that we know our stuff, and they even admit, grudgingly, that they have improved their writing. Nevertheless, when they give us a general evaluation, the Rhetoric Department always comes in last in comparison to the other four courses.

Since we should be doing more about reading and study techniques and since our progress in the first semester lets us take some chances in the second semester, we have begun experimenting with several forms of content. With one-third of our faculty continuing to work with anthology-type models and thus acting as control group, two teachers and one-third of our students are going heavily into the "content" of a writing course—more semantics, more linguistics, and more of the history and nature of language and epistemology. Another third of the classes is working with a social content, based on a collection of essays about social history, including art, politics, customs, and science.

A second problem is that the student load for each rhetoric teacher is heavy. Each instructor teaches four sections, with twenty-eight to thirty students in each. Each teacher has a contact load of nine hours, meeting each section twice a week and all students together once.

The administration has tried to help. For several years we experimented with an intern system which provided each professor with a three-fifths-time graduate student. This did lighten the load, but too often we got idiosyncratic grading from interns who could not work into our system of standardized ratings; then too, we were self-conscious about violating an original tenet of the college, that all teaching would be by full-time professionals.

For several years we assigned two rhetoric teachers per team, giving us a 60-1 ratio, as recommended by the National Council of Teachers of English. To our surprise this had many disadvantages. Few rhetoric teachers were able to work in pairs, partly because of different temperaments and philosophies, but also because of different student needs. When students saw these differences, they complained of inequality. Our colleagues in other departments, feeling that we had a lighter load than they did, left all the writing business to us. And with the cost of rhetoric instruction doubled, we had to face the fact that the system was just not cost effective. We could not justify the system with our Gain Studies: just as many students failed, just as many continued to have problems, and no more succeeded.

We are now trying to help lessen the teaching load by slicing off part of the writing problem. We have employed a writing specialist to work out a program to help especially needy students in grammar, spelling, and punctuation. We are also getting help from our colleagues, who more and more are assigning carefully designed writing exercises. In addition to providing students an opportunity to demonstrate mastery of course content, these exercises also put students through the demanding requirements of analysis, synthesis, structure, development, and expression, the mastery of which has been the rhetoric goal.

A third problem which concerns us is that writing progress does not hold up as well as we might expect after our students leave us. Our students do relatively well in advanced writing classes, and they write as well as the students from other writing programs, but as sophomores, our students often do turn in embarrassing papers to our CBS colleagues. We recognize this deterioration is endemic; but we keep telling ourselves that if we were truly doing our job, we would be giving students the principles and motivation to want to write well and the ability to police their own work. We have added a sophomore remedial course to which students are assigned by teachers from other departments. A study by a doctoral candidate has given us suggestions about the kind of principles (particularly those about revision) that seem to stick best with students. And we continue to work on the problem.

A development which helps us endure our problems is the improving nature of our students. Most of them in September are still vastly unskilled as writers, but their precollege attitude is healthy. They rarely know how to study, but—in contrast to the past—they want to learn. They realize that writing competence is highly relevant to their future well-being. They appreciate the pointed diagnosis we give them, they like the individual attention, and they work. They are justifiably proud of their improvement. And most of them are learning to write reasonably well, and that's why we are in business.

III Evaluation and Testing

7 A Successful Placement Test for Basic Writing

Nancy W. Johnson
Northern Virginia Community College

Johnson grapples with the problem of composition placement testing. Although admitting that writing samples provide the most accurate measure of student writing ability, she demonstrates how an objective test can be constructed that will be valid and reliable for placement purposes.

Placing students at the appropriate English composition level to increase their chances of success is a recurrent problem at colleges and universities nationwide. Every curriculum that acknowledges individual differences and capabilities among students implies a determination of how such differences will be identified. The problem is further complicated by reports that SAT scores, when available, may not serve as accurate indicators of students' composing abilities and by the open-door admissions policy of many community and junior colleges.

Two major approaches to this problem of placement have been tried, albeit with limited success. The more common approach, and the one favored by English teachers, at least in theory, is to require incoming students to write an essay to be evaluated by the teacher. This approach is frequently modified in the name of objective grading to require that each student paper be read more than once. The drawback of this approach is the time required to collect and score essays. A second approach is to require incoming students to take a grammar test. The drawback of this approach is that such tests seldom incorporate the rhetorical elements necessary in written composition, and, therefore, do not accurately reflect the students' writing abilities.

Increased enrollment and limited registration timetables seem to dictate a move toward an easily administered and easily scored placement instrument. An objective test is an apparent answer to this need, but in light of the drawbacks of the other alternatives, the essential question is "Can an objective test give an accurate evaluation of the skills a student must have to perform successfully in a composition class?" Our experiences in placement testing at Northern Virginia Community College lead us to respond to this question positively.

There are some basic assumptions about the nature of composition and the evaluation of compositions which must be agreed upon before a placement instrument can be constructed. First, it must be agreed that composition is a process and, as such, may be studied. Second, it must be agreed that the scientific study of the process by qualified researchers can reveal the inherent parts which make up the process. Finally, it must be agreed that experienced composition teachers are best qualified to examine the composition process and to identify those qualities which combine to produce good writing. With these basic assumptions in mind, the N.V.C.C. English Department and the Department of Developmental Studies began work on an English placement test for entering students.

Constructing the Test Instrument

The first pedagogical consideration in constructing a placement test was to define the population to be tested. By analyzing demographic data on N.V.C.C. students, indicating the relationship between our students and those attending the four other campuses of N.V.C.C. on the basis of enrollment, curriculum, student status, race, sex, and age, we were able to construct accurate profiles of our student body. In addition, student profiles were compared with those of community college students nationwide.[1] This information was useful in helping us to formulate test items by identifying characteristics of our students which might indicate interests and attitudes. For example, the average age of our students was 25.8 years, considerably older than the "average" freshman class nationally.

The next step was to select a representative sample of the population for study to determine how our students wrote. Since the demographic data revealed a highly diverse student body, we began by identifying broad registration trends. Students were selected from three categories: (1) those attending classes during prime time (10 a.m. to 3 p.m., MWF), (2) those attending classes on Tuesday and Thursday, and (3) those attending classes at night. Approximately equal numbers of students in each category were selected from the following courses: Developmental English (a remedial course carrying no transfer credit), English Composition I, and English Composition II (both three-credit transfer courses). We reasoned that we would learn more about entering students' writing abilities by comparing their writing samples with those of

Placement Test for Basic Writing

students who enrolled in remedial English or who had already successfully completed one writing course than by studying entering students' writing samples in isolation. The student sample thus covered the range of competency levels as well as the span of enrollment patterns.

Students participating in the sampling were given fifty minutes to write an impromptu essay on the first day of class. The papers covered three modes of discourse—narration, description, and argumentation—and three topics—school, self, and society—totaling nine topic-mode combinations. The nine topics were as follows:[2]

1. Think of a critical event in your life—an incident or situation that had an important effect on you. It could be something that happened yesterday or when you were five years old. It could have happened someplace exciting or at home while you were eating dinner. It might have taught you an important lesson. Write an essay about this event in such a way that its importance is made clear.
2. You are many different people. There is the you that goes to school, the you with your friends, the you that does the thing you enjoy best. Which of them is the real you? Decide on a situation or activity in which you are most yourself. "I am a dreamer," "I am a ball player," "I am a dancer," etc.
3. In the past few years, you have probably thought a lot about parents—what they did right, what they might have done better. You may be a parent yourself now or in the future. Taking this as your topic, "If I had a son" or "If I had a daughter," explain what you would hope to do for your child. Explain why you would do it.
4. Recently you went through registration. Such an experience generally produces lasting impressions. Write an essay about your experience.
5. Between classes, you probably spend time somewhere on campus. Try to describe the place accurately; concentrate on looks, smell, and sound.
6. Some people think that schools should be open all year long. If the schools were open, students and teachers would be able to choose when they would have their vacations, in the summer as usual or in the fall, winter, or spring. Decide how you feel about year-round school. Then write down your feelings, making sure to tell why you feel the way you do.
7. Many important events have occurred during your lifetime—the moon landing, the assassination of John Kennedy, the earthquake in Los Angeles, for example. Pick an important event and write about it for someone who has never heard about it before.
8. Everyone has different ideas about the word *American* and what it means. Write about an event or scene which you feel is typically American. Use anything you would like, a football game, a

hamburger, a television show, anything. Write about it so that somebody who did not live in America would know all about it.
9. Imagine that a large company near you has been found to be seriously polluting a local river. Some people have been talking about closing the company down until something can be done about the pollution. If the company is closed down, many people will be out of work. Write your ideas about whether to shut down the company or not. Be sure to indicate why you feel the way you do.

Students were randomly assigned to topic-mode combinations to assure that the papers collected were typical performances rather than the best performances which could be expected if students were allowed to select their own topics. All nine topics were represented at each proficiency level and in each time block.

Seventy randomly selected papers from the sample were read holistically by four composition teachers to determine the levels of language achievement of our students. Holistic grading, also called general impression grading, requires that a paper be read from beginning to end and judged according to overall quality. We used holistic grading because it is faster than analytic grading, which requires more specification, while proving equally reliable. Studies by Cast, Coward, Nisbet, Ravan, and others have shown that the crucial factor in essay grading is a clear articulation, prior to grading, of what norms are being applied by the judges, not the grading scale itself.[3] Judges were asked to classify papers using a three-point scale: (1) students who were in need of remedial work; (2) students who were ready to enroll in first quarter composition; and (3) students who were prepared to enroll in second quarter composition.

The initial reading session was followed by a discussion of the relative merits of each group of papers. Judges were asked to describe the papers in each group, indicating similarities among papers within a group and differences among groups. Not surprisingly, the judges placed many of the same papers in the same group, although their reasons for doing so varied. In other words, judges were able to agree upon a level of acceptable writing although their perspectives differed. While we sought unanimity in classifying papers into groups, we did not specify what criteria each judge should use.

This discussion resulted in the specification of seven areas which, collectively, could be used to describe good writing. These seven areas were (1) content, (2) organization, (3) overall development, (4) diction, (5) style, (6) mechanical errors, and (7) spelling. Judges then agreed upon descriptive statements of each category at each writing proficiency level, and these statements were listed in a table of specifications (see Table 1).

Table 1

Table of Specifications

	Group 1	Group 2	Group 3
Content	Barely discernible; papers say little	Largely superficial	Goes beyond superficial; writer often reaches logical conclusions which show some insight
Organization	Little or no sequence or central idea; papers often brief	Discernible pattern; some feeling for a central idea	Appropriate coordination, subordination in developing strong central idea
Overall development	Fragmented ideas, very few details; both ideas, details may be repetitious, inappropriate	Use of detail is appropriate, sufficient	Generalizations supported with extensive, concrete detail
Diction	Range of word choice limited; misuse of words common	Range of word choice adequate; some awareness of connotations	Range of word choice good; words chosen show awareness of connotations that fit needs of context
Style	Not displayed consistently enough to be identified	Inconsistent in tone, erratic; uninspired, uninspiring	Awareness of audience, deliberate use of tone, conscious choice of other rhetorical devices to enhance, sustain meaning, interest
Mechanics	Consistent problems with deletions of verb endings, run-ons, fragments, shifting verb tenses	Minor errors, occasional major problems; grammatical errors do not impede flow of paper	Generally free of mechanical errors
Spelling	Many misspellings of common words	Occasional misspellings of difficult words; misspellings do not obscure recognition of intended words	Spelling errors rare

This method provided a descriptive statement about where students actually are in their use of language rather than a prescriptive statement about where they might be expected to be and therefore reaffirmed our original hypothesis that placement tests must be derived from the writing samples of a particular student body and must be based on local norms. The table of specifications was then used to score fifty-four additional papers to see if it could be consistently applied; the results showed that it could be.

Studies by Braddock et al., Godshalk et al., and Diederich show that agreement, or reader reliability, may be achieved and increased by keeping writers anonymous, by clearly defining the measuring tool (in this case our table of specifications), and by increasing the number of competent readers.[4] A competent reader is one who is capable of distinguishing the two areas of composition, grammar and rhetoric, and of judging when they are effectively applied. Assuming that a reader is capable of this judgment, she or he becomes the logical choice as a writer of test items. Thus, the distinction between the reader and the writer of test items is one of operations, not of persons, and the specification of the kinds of knowledge necessary is the same for both reader and tester.

The Claims of the Test Designer

The specification of the tester's knowledge requires a conceptualization of a theory of grammar and a theory of rhetoric. An important pedagogical consideration, then, is the capacities and limitations of the designer of the test in conceptualizing these theories. The function of grammatical theory is to provide a full and accurate description of the structure of the language; the function of rhetorical theory is to provide resources for the effective use of language. Together, language and its use constitute what is to be tested.

The designer of a test claims knowledge of a set of norms or standards of grammatical correctness which are present in speech constructs and which are responsible for conveying meaning. However, in a language which is alive, speakers who use the language may deviate from its norms; such deviation produces a unique semantic effect. To say whether the effect is good or not, one must know what the grammatical norms are and what the effect is or is likely to be. Therefore, a test constructed solely in terms of grammatical norms does not provide for actual usage. The flaw in the procedure is obvious. While readers or testers must have an idea of what constitutes correctness in English prior to making judgments, they must recognize that these norms alone do not determine effectiveness.

A more logical procedure is to combine the theoretical aspect—especially as that provides for a distinction between grammar and rhetoric—with the practical aspect, the evaluation of actual student writing, prior to test construction. Such a procedure is highly informative, since it places a conceptualized set of norms in relation to a set of essays. The result must undoubtedly be a revised hierarchy of student needs if standards of correctness and effectiveness are to be achieved. Test questions will then reflect what teachers should teach in composition classes, if actual usage is to approach standards of correctness derived from grammar and standards of correctness derived from rhetoric.

The Responses of the Test-taker

A further pedagogical consideration in test construction is determining the types of responses which students are expected to make. To do so, we must first examine the relationship between the student and the subject matter. In writing an essay the student combines the complex acts of thinking and writing. In this situation "thinking is a direct movement of subject matter to a completing issue,"[5] the recording of thoughts or feelings in correct and effective sentences. Thus, in writing an essay the student makes deliberate grammatical and rhetorical choices which express his or her ideas; i.e., the student develops a method, an "effective direction of subject matter to desired results."[6] By writing an essay which is grammatically correct and rhetorically effective, the student displays the ability to use the arts of grammar and rhetoric. However, a superior end product does not clearly specify the kinds of knowledge of grammar and rhetoric which the student possesses, although a poor end product may indicate areas of incompetence due to lack of knowledge. Knowledge requires that "two conditions are satisfied: the truth condition and the evidence condition."[7] Students make grammatical and rhetorical mistakes because they lack knowledge of grammar and rhetoric, but they may believe that they have knowledge in these areas. In a testing situation, the tester must be able to distinguish between knowledge and belief and, further, to discriminate among types of knowledge, which may be divided into the logically distinct areas of "knowing how," "knowing the," "knowing that," and "knowing why."[8] The first may only be tested directly by requiring a student to write. However, by testing the other three types of knowledge, one may construct an objective test that will provide the same, or nearly the same, information about a student's knowledge of grammar and rhetoric that a writing sample will.

The Functional Level: "Knowing the"

"Knowing the" rules of spelling, punctuation, and grammar, and the definitions of words identifies a student's knowledge of the functional level of language. Such knowledge is essential for written communication and may be tested directly by asking a student to select the correctly spelled word, the correctly punctuated sentence, the sentence from among fragments and vice versa, and the correct word for use in a sentence. "Knowing the" connotations of words identifies a student's ability to make one of the simplest rhetorical choices, word choice. To test this knowledge, a student might be asked to select the most effective word for use in a sentence or to select the word that is used incorrectly. For example, one test item on an earlier form of the N.V.C.C. test asked students which of the underscored words was used incorrectly in the following sentence: "<u>Two</u> years of <u>algebra</u> <u>is</u> the <u>requisite</u> for this course." Another test item asked students to choose the best word to fit into the following sentence: " 'He took _____ to that remark.' (a) acception; (b) exception; (c) exemption; (d) accession."

The Application Level: "Knowing that"

Closely allied to "knowing the" rules is "knowing that" the rules have been correctly applied. "Knowing that" a word is correctly used or that a paragraph is well structured identifies a student's knowledge of grammar. For instance, a student should know that words in sentences form relationships. The relationships are both grammatical and rhetorical, with phrases and clauses providing amplification or qualification to basic sentence parts. To test knowledge of relationships, a student might be asked to identify the most important piece of information in a sentence. For example, one test item asked students to read the following sentence and pick out the most important piece of information: " 'As Mr. Nilson, well known in the City, opened the window of his dressing room on Campden Hill, he experienced a peculiar sweetish sensation in the back of his throat and a feeling of emptiness just under his fifth rib.'[9] (a) Mr. Nilson was well known. (b) Mr. Nilson experienced a feeling of emptiness. (c) Mr. Nilson lived on Campden Hill. (d) Mr. Nilson smelled something sweet." A student should also know that concrete words are usually preferable to abstract ones for reinforcing meaning. To test this knowledge, a student might be asked to identify a sentence which does or does not add support to a paragraph.

"Knowing that" a word or sentence is effective identifies a student's intermediate knowledge of rhetoric. To test this knowledge, a student might be asked to identify an appropriate word or sentence in a particular context or to select the sentence whose parts are arranged most effectively from a group of grammatically correct sentences. For example, in one test item students were told that a young woman being interviewed for a job had a choice of making one of the following statements, and they were asked to select the one her prospective employer would find most convincing. The choices were as follows: "(a) I am prepared to work hard for the company. (b) I am a hard worker. I always have been. (c) I received an award for hard work from my last employer. (d) I offered meritorious service and hard work to my last employer."

The Judgment Level: "Knowing why"

"Knowing why" a sentence is confusing identifies a student's awareness of grammatical alternatives. Competent student writers should know that they have options and what the options are. They exemplify their command of the English language in a test situation by indicating why the choice of certain options is desirable. They should be able to explain why they do what they do. Since language is a system, the student writer must know the parts of the system, how the parts function within the system, and how the whole of the system functions. To test this latter knowledge, a student might be asked to identify the sentence whose meaning is most clear from among sentences whose meanings are obscured by haphazard placement of phrases and clauses. For example, one test item asked students to select the sentence which stated the idea most clearly from the following choices: "(a) Hiding in a vacant building and using a high-powered rifle, Lee Harvey Oswald was accused of assassinating President Kennedy. (b) Lee Harvey Oswald was accused of assassinating President Kennedy, hiding in a vacant building and using a high-powered rifle. (c) Assassinating President Kennedy, Lee Harvey Oswald was accused of hiding in a vacant building and using a high-powered rifle. (d) Lee Harvey Oswald was accused of hiding in a vacant building and using a high-powered rifle to assassinate President Kennedy."

"Knowing why" certain words or examples are effective with certain audiences identifies a student's knowledge of the larger rhetorical elements, i.e., invention and arrangement. To test this knowledge, a student might be asked to explain why a sentence or a paragraph should be developed along certain lines. A student might also be asked to identify the reason why a sentence does not add support to a paragraph or what is wrong with a sentence as it relates to other sentences in a paragraph. For example, one test item read: "In an essay arguing in favor of neutering pets, a student stated that young children can by psychologically scarred by watching pets procreate and give birth. What is wrong with this idea as it relates to the paper's topic? (a) The statement is based on an emotional appeal. (b) There could be no evidence to support such a statement. (c) The statement is only vaguely related to the topic. (d) The student does not explain the nature of the psychological scars."

Thus, it is possible to construct multiple-choice items in which students are asked to perform mental activities which closely approximate those required in actual writing. Further, if the categories to be tested have been taken from student papers and these papers have been used for reference in constructing test items, the relation between actual writing and test items is reinforced. For specific information on writing good objective test items, see Bormuth, Gronlund, and Thorndike.[10]

Validity and Reliability

Ideally, an effective placement test must demonstrate validity. A test may be said to be valid to the extent to which it does what it was designed to do, in this case to place students accurately in composition classes. The validity of most objective tests is determined by norm-reference, i.e., by comparing a student's score with those of other students. According to a 1975 National Council of Teachers of English study, *Common Sense and Testing in English,* "the norm cannot be considered a 'fair' basis for comparison of groups in any case unless the tested population is very similar in all respects to the normative population—a condition which rarely exists."[11] A more useful type of validity is by criterion-reference, i.e., establishing some criterion and then determining the relationship between the test and this criterion. Thus, the best criterion for a writing placement test is a writing sample. This was the criterion used to validate the N.V.C.C. English Qualifying Examination.

During field testing of the N.V.C.C. exam, students answered objective questions and wrote an essay on an assigned topic, one of the nine topics used in collecting the original sample papers. These new papers were scored by three composition teachers, using the table of specifications as their criteria. Readers were "trained" on the original papers to insure reader reliability. The scores received on the papers were correlated with the scores received on the objective tests. The correlation between the essay score and the total test was .65 for Form A of the test and .62 for Form B, which are both significant at the .01 level. Test items which did not correlate highly with essay scores or with other test items attempting to measure the same category (for instance, content) were dropped from the test. This criterion-referencing allowed us to predict a student's essay score merely by looking at his or her score on the objective test.

A second type of validity is content validity, the adequacy of the test to sample the population it purports to represent. The N.V.C.C. placement test fulfills the requirements for content validity. The procedures described earlier for collecting and scoring the initial essays identified the requirements necessary for entrance into the freshman English sequence by enumerating the subject matter aspects of good writing. These aspects were described in the table of specifications used in constructing test items.

In addition to demonstrating validity, a placement instrument must also demonstrate reliability, which Diederich defines as the "amount of agreement between two sets of independent measures of the same characteristic in the same student, taken at about the same time."[12] One recognized type of reliability is the measurement of internal consistency of the test itself.[13] Another form of reliability is the measurement of stability and equivalence by the test-retest with equivalent forms of the test method.[14] Both types of reliability were shown to be present in the N.V.C.C. placement test.

What is perhaps more important to an English department constructing a placement test is the relationship between student performance on the test and performance in the composition class. Since we began administering our placement test prior to registration and using only this objective test to place students, we have observed four significant classroom trends.

First, classes are more homogeneous. Second, there is a higher successful completion rate. An analysis of grade distributions for five consecutive quarters prior to the administration of the English Qualifying Examination showed that a minimum of 30.35 percent of the students enrolled in first quarter freshman composition either failed, withdrew, or did not complete the course. During the fall quarter, 1977, the latest quarter for which grade distributions are available, only 24.4 percent of the students enrolled in first-quarter freshman composition either failed, withdrew, or did not complete the course. (For a breakdown by quarter, see Table 2.) It should be noted that during the first two quarters after the English Qualifying Examination was implemented, test administration procedures were noticeably inadequate. During these two quarters, over 50 percent of the students appearing on the first grade roll had not taken the test. A large number of these students were withdrawn from classes because they subsequently failed the test.

Third, there has been a drastic reduction in the number of students who go through drop/add. Previously, students were given a writing sample on the first day of class and were advised, if the essay did not meet the instructor's standards of competency, to drop the class and enroll in remedial English. This method of placement resulted in many students

Table 2

Grade Distributions of Students
Who Did Not Successfully Complete
First Freshman Composition Course

Quarter	Failure (%)	Withdrawal/ Incomplete/ Re-enroll (%)	Total Percentage (%)	Number of Students
Fall '73[1]	6.18	26.02	32.2	2,264
Winter '74[1]	4.79	31.24	36.03	938
Spring '74[1]	3.06	40.23	43.29	522
Summer '74[1]	2.23	28.12	30.35	313
Fall '74[1]	4.65	26.34	30.99	2,084
Winter '75	5.08	35.58	42.5	846
Spring '75	1.36	37.11	38.47	512
Summer '75	2.28	26.38	28.66	307
Fall '75	4.33	21.63	25.96	1,803
Winter '76	2.2	32.8	35.0	761
Spring '76	3.6	33.2	37.4	495
Summer '76	0.0	23.8	23.8	121
Fall '76	3.5	18.0	21.5	1,587
Winter '77	8.7	20.6	29.3	769
Spring '77	8.0	22.4	30.4	470
Summer '77	5.7	22.4	28.1	261
Fall '77	6.2	18.2	24.4	1,610

Source: Grade Distribution Analyses, Office of Institutional Research, Northern Virginia Community College.

1. Prior to administration of placement examination.

being sent to drop/add, further encumbering this process and requiring valuable time for classes to stabilize. Since it is short and easily scored, the English Qualifying Examination is administered before registration, thereby simplifying the drop/add process. Although most teachers continue to give an impromptu essay during the first class meeting and retain the right to recommend that a student withdraw on the basis of that essay, an average of only 1 percent of students who have passed the objective test are advised to withdraw from a class per quarter.

Fourth, there is a significant relationship between the score on the test and the grade received at the end of the quarter. The large number of students who were enrolled in first-quarter freshman composition without having taken the test provided a control group with which to compare students placed by the test (see Table 3). Of course, it is impossible to predict how well these students would have done had they taken the test. Nevertheless, it is interesting to note that the completion rate of students placed by the test is consistently higher than that of students who did not take the test.

Table 3

Comparison of Successful Completion Rates of Students Passing English Qualifying Exam and Students Not Taking Exam

Quarter	Students Passing Exam	Students Not Taking Exam
Winter '75	65.04 (389)	54.48 (457)
Spring '75	75.35 (211)	51.83 (301)
Spring '76	62.83 (261)	59.47 (153)
Summer '76	80.43 (138)	63.53 (85)
Fall '76	78.83 (1,020)	65.58 (141)
Winter '77	69.87 (313)	57.0 (100)
Spring '77	70.55 (292)	63.78 (127)
Summer '77	76.58 (158)	65.15 (66)
Fall '77	78.81 (926)	63.87 (175)

Source: English Department records, Northern Virginia Community College.

Note: Figure in parentheses is number of students.

Conclusions

The results of the studies done on this placement test, reported only briefly here,[15] suggest five conclusions which help to clarify the state of placement testing in English:

1. A writing sample is the best, though not the most efficient, measure of writing ability.
2. Readers can agree on the worth of writing samples after testing their conceptualizations of what constitutes correctness in usage.
3. Comparing conceptualizations to actual performance reveals categories to be tested and areas to be taught.
4. Objective questions may be constructed from these categories for the sake of efficacy.
5. An objective test thus constructed and correlated with actual writing performances serves as a time-effective method for student placement if the population is clearly defined.

This study may serve as a model for other institutions who are dissatisfied with their current placement procedures or who have no procedure for placement. The procedure described here returns the judgment of competence in composition to those who are most skilled in the subject matter, English teachers, where it rightly belongs.

8 Choosing or Creating an Appropriate Writing Test

Rexford Brown
National Assessment of Educational Progress

> Brown begins by listing the questions an instructor should answer before designing or purchasing a test of basic writing. He then discusses the strengths and weaknesses of various types of essay and objective tests and the differences between testing and comprehensive evaluation of writing.

The clamor of education's many constituents for various kinds of information about basic writing skills makes the task of selecting appropriate tests or evaluation programs both complicated and confusing. Teachers, students, school superintendents, deans, graduate schools, parents, and the business community all demand different kinds of information congruent with their needs and their perceptions about language and the nature of evidence. This essay is intended to clarify the advantages and disadvantages of various approaches to the assessment of writing. But the reader will have to participate in the clarification by answering three sets of questions about the intended use of a test, its content, and the resources available for its creation or purchase.

The Uses of Tests

The first set of questions concerns the intended use of a test. A discussion of each question follows the list.

1. Do you primarily want to predict the future writing success of your students?
2. Do you seek to place students at certain levels or to excuse them from certain courses?
3. Do you want to diagnose writing problems?
4. Do you want to establish mastery?
5. Do you want to compare your students, as a group, to others?

6. Do you primarily want to describe your students' writing?
7. Do you want to measure growth in student writing skills?
8. Do you want to conduct any long-term research on writing?
9. Do you expect a test to teach as it tests?
10. Do you want all of the above?

(1) Prediction

If you want to predict the future success of your students, most standardized multiple-choice tests of "writing," i.e., usage, punctuation, capitalization, spelling, and recognition of errors in other people's writing, will predict reasonably well.[1] If you couple such test scores as the ACT or the College Boards with reading scores and information about students' home environments, your predictions will be even more accurate. This approach costs little, but it also reveals little about specific strengths and weaknesses in students' writing.[2]

(2) Placement

Commercial standardized tests—e.g., the College English Placement Test, the College Placement Test in English Composition, or the Missouri College English Test—are somewhat helpful as gross indicators of competence. With such tests you can rank-order students and divide them into groups targeted for various levels of instruction. However, that approach by itself is unsatisfactory; knowing nothing absolute about the *writing* of the students, you could well be assigning the same work to people who achieved identical scores on a test but labor under very different writing problems. Prudence suggests you assign an essay or two and evaluate it independently of the multiple-choice test. The College English Placement Test, in fact, offers an optional essay.

Holistic scoring of essays has proven to be an efficient, relatively cheap, and reliable way of rank-ordering papers for such purposes as placement, college admissions, and so on. This approach, used for decades by the College Boards, involves training readers to respond to essays with an overall (holistic) judgment of their quality, without attending to their constituent parts or such matters as usage, grammar, and spelling. These matters are important only insofar as they contribute to the overall impact of the paper upon a reader who is reading, judging quickly (without discussion), and moving on to the next paper. A placement decision based upon both a test score and a holistic essay ranking is more defensible than a decision based on either alone, because the combination generally results in higher reliability estimates. Holistic scorings are easier to conduct, cheaper, and less time consuming than many people suppose. Once cooperating faculty members have been trained (which takes three to four hours), they can read an essay every few minutes, especially if the papers are short by design. With careful selection of training papers and an attention to details (e.g., preparing reader packets, designing an efficient system for recording and tallying scores, etc.), a group of teachers can streamline holistic scoring sessions and even create a pleasant working atmosphere for all involved. Information about holistic scoring is readily available from the Educational Testing Service in Princeton, New Jersey, or from many state departments of education or assessment.

(3) Diagnosis

Subscores on standardized multiple-choice tests are indirect and too gross to be useful for practical diagnosis. The most any standardized test can tell you is that a student's subscore on "sentence sensitivity" or "paragraph arrangement" or "usage" or "punctuation" was low. Since the student was asked not to write, but to find errors in other people's writing, you do not know if the student's own writing will reflect problems in the subskill. Furthermore, there are so many reasons for making punctuation errors (including carelessness, bidialectical interference, or ignorance about the nature of a sentence) that news of a low subscore in punctuation is not very helpful; you will have to do further evaluation before you can determine what course of action will best meet a student's needs. Holistic scoring of essays is not diagnostic, either; it is simply another way of rank-ordering papers. Student-specific diagnostic information comes only from the close examination of student writing. Examiners must scrutinize papers written in several discourse modes and under varying situations before they can hope to pinpoint problems. A successful creative writer, for instance, may have special problems writing descriptive or analytic prose that calls for more rigid logical relationships and different conventions of presentation; unless he or she is asked to write in several modes, this fact may escape notice.

Diagnosis depends upon the teacher's knowledge of what to look for. Can the teacher characterize writing problems specifically? Or is he or she given to writing "awk" or "amb" or "unclear" in the margin and leaving the responsibility for diagnosis with the puzzled student? Can the teacher determine whether a particular problem was a consequence of deficient understanding of sentence structure or simple haste? Was a sentence awkward because the writer could not form complex sentences or because the writer tried to begin the sentence with something that should have been subordinated and got tangled up trying to subordinate the main clause? When is an apparent punctuation problem really a failure to hear a complete sentence? When is a tense shift an editorial failure, and when is it a confusion of point of view? When is a generally bad paper the result of an attitude problem, not a skill difficulty?

All of us who diagnose writing must answer these and many other questions if we hope to be helpful. And we must see to it that there is a close relationship between what we look for in diagnosis and what we teach, for it would be useless to diagnose a problem in speaker-audience relationship if class time is devoted entirely to grammar. And it would be equally profitless to diagnose a problem with syntax if you do not intend to teach enough grammar to enable your students to understand what is wrong with their sentences.

Rubric essay scoring systems, such as the E.T.S. Composition Evaluation Scales (CES) designed by Diederich, can be aids to diagnosis.[3] The CES breaks essay evaluation into eight separate components: ideas, organization, wording, flavor, usage, punctuation, spelling, and handwriting. Each component is ranked on a five-point scale, with ideas and organization receiving double weight. This forces a grader to narrow an essay's problems down to general categories, and that is at least a start toward diagnosis. However, once one has told a student that his or her problems lie in organization, one is obliged to be more specific still.

The National Assessment's "primary trait" scoring represents an even more specific diagnostic approach.[4] To employ this approach, the test designer must first decide what is to be learned and then construct the assignment and scoring guide so that it will be learned. For instance, let us say a high school teacher wants to know whether students can write a formal letter that persuades through the use of argument supported by concrete detail. The teacher must first construct an appropriate formal writing situation (e.g., a letter to a school board) and an issue students are likely to have feelings about (e.g., smoking in school, cafeteria food, public displays of affection). The teacher must then describe in detail four levels of writing quality. First-level papers do not adhere to the conventions of formal letter writing or do not produce any arguments for or against the relevant issue. Such letters would not persuade anyone of anything. Level two papers may show knowledge of formal conventions and may produce one argument for a position, but the argument is undeveloped and unsupported with concrete details. These papers show some savvy, but they, too, would not be persuasive. Level three papers clearly adhere to the appropriate conventions, demonstrate adequate audience awareness, produce several arguments for a position, and support at least one of the arguments with concrete details. They are likely to be read sympathetically. Level four papers go beyond the level three papers in their sensitivity to audience, the ingenuity of their arguments, the amount of concrete detail, and the use of that detail in support of arguments. Each of these levels must be described in much more detail, of course; the formal conventions must be listed, the conditions for each level must be carefully thought through and explicitly stated. The point is that in this approach you design your writing task to elicit specific skills and you evaluate to see if they are in evidence. Many other things may be in evidence, as well, and you can examine or even evaluate them after you have evaluated the student's control of the primary rhetorical skill you were focusing upon. Afterwards, all students can be told exactly why they received their scores and what they must do to raise them.

(4) Mastery

Few of us ever master writing, and even if we did, no one test would ever be sufficient to prove our mastery. When this word is used, it generally refers to mastery of low-level component skills like punctuation, capacity to write complete sentences, spelling, and so on. Unfortunately, one can master these skills one at a time and still be a terrible writer.

Teachers should be leery of tests that purport to measure mastery in multiple-choice format. To begin with, you cannot establish mastery by indirect measures, i.e., by having students demonstrate skill in finding errors in other people's writing, as they are required to do in multiple-choice tests. Success on such tests is only evidence of mastery of proofreading, not writing. And you cannot establish mastery when the students' sphere of action is limited to only four possible remedies for sentence problems; these approaches are too removed from the real world of writing to establish anything significant. If you want to establish mastery of low-level components of writing, you must try to discover how these components are handled in the context of real writing, not just in isolation. This means that in addition to sentence-level drill, you must have students write whole pieces of discourse and you must infer mastery of low-level skills from the evidence that students use higher-level skills.

(5) Comparisons

Any nationally normed test can establish how one set of students fared vis-à-vis others in the country—at least in terms of percentile ranks, stanines, or grade equivalents. It is not clear how this information relates to the teaching of writing, but it is information many people seem to crave. If we knew exactly why one group of students performs differently from another, comparative data could have direct application to education. In our present state of ignorance, however, the primary purpose of such comparative approaches is to document educational inequities and formulate policy. As important as this is for the policy maker, it is information teachers cannot yet profit from directly. Anyone using nationally normed data should carefully read its accompanying technical information about the sample design, date of last norming, and so on. Many standardized tests are not regularly normed, and you could be unwittingly ranking your students against populations that no longer exist.

(6) Description

Description is interesting in itself and often useful as a step toward evaluation. There are many things one might want to describe about one's writers: their attitudes about writing, their prewriting behavior, their editing strategies, rewriting strategies, and so on. And there are dozens of things one can describe about their essays: sentence length and type, syntactic maturity, common problems, cognitive strategies, concreteness of words, number of words, amount of embedding, kinds of modification, and more. Quantitative data about number of words per T-unit, number of words per subordinate clause, relative clauses per one hundred T-units, and so on have been instrumental in the development of writing programs that stress sentence-combining activities to improve certain writing skills. Teachers interested in this approach, and in possession of the resources to analyze essays quantitatively, might consult such guides as Dixon's "Indexes of Syntactic Maturity"[5] or Mellon's "Factors of Syntactic Fluency."[6] The O'Donnell and Hunt "Syntactic Maturity Test" (SMT)[7] and the Dauterman "Syntactic Maturity Test for Narrative Writing" (SMTNW)[8] provide syntactic maturity information without requiring essay analysis. (All are available through the ERIC system.) A National Assessment report, *Writing Mechanics, 1969-1974*, demonstrates the advantages of combining descriptive analysis with evaluative judgment.[9] One finds that the better essays differ substantially from the poorer ones in quantitative ways and that these differences lead to concrete instructional strategies for improving writing.

(7) Growth

Short-term growth is not easy to discern in a skill as complicated as writing. Over a period of months, one student might learn to combine his ideas into smoother sentences, another might become a much better editor of her own writing, and a third might discover profound personal satisfaction in expressive writing; but these gains may not be reflected in their class essays (especially if they have not written many), or they may be overshadowed by lingering problems with diction, punctuation, or audience. A teacher might notice a general improvement but be unable to say specifically what accounts for the change. These difficulties are compounded by the observation that advances in writing inevitably bring to light new problems. As students deal with higher-level challenges, they trade old problems for new ones. If the different character of these errors goes unrecognized, it may appear that they have made no advances at all.

An improved score on a multiple-choice test is equivocal evidence of change in writing skill, given that scores on such tests can be boosted in many ways and given their gross coverage of minor component skills. One-shot essay examination is risky, as well. We are all capable of bad days or bad responses to particular essay topics. An improved grade on an essay administered both before and after course instruction may reflect growth, but it may also indicate that students write better essays about a topic after they have tried it once for practice. If pre- and post-course essays are different, the results may vary because the essays are not of comparable difficulty.

Some people quantitatively analyze "before" and "after" essays and consult various indices of syntactic maturity to discern improvement. Unfortunately, even if the subordination ratio of an essay moved from 0.299 to 0.334 and the mean T-unit length stretched from 11.9 to 15.3, the "after" essay could be terrible. Simple-minded application of "maturity" indices would be irresponsible.

In *Measuring Growth in English* Diederich provides a means of looking at improvement across an entire high school by pooling the papers of ninth, tenth, eleventh, and twelfth graders and conducting a blind holistic scoring.[10] The results generally show improvement from class to class in the percentages of good essays—evidence that students do improve with age and instruction. It would be interesting to see if there is a similar progression between the freshman and senior years of college. The National Assessment has also conducted blind holistic scorings in which papers written at two different times were pooled. Having no way of knowing whether a given paper was written in 1969 or 1974, readers were forced to apply the same criteria to all. When the scoring was over, it emerged that the readers judged the 1969 papers, as a group, somewhat better than the 1974 papers. Quantitative analysis of the papers later revealed substantial differences that undoubtedly affected the readers' responses.

The National Assessment combination of holistic evaluation and descriptive analysis is a potent way of assessing growth or decline in writing skills, but, like the Diederich approach, it is used primarily for assessing large groups of people and looking for gross changes over relatively long periods. Instructors interested in measuring the growth of individuals over short periods will need several essays, each of which reveals something the others do not. If one "before" essay requires concrete details and elaborations, it is simple to determine whether or not a similar "after" essay contains more concrete language and more supporting detail. If another "before" essay requires the establishing and detailing of relationships between facts randomly presented to the writers, the instructor can repeat the exercise and look for those specific things as well. The trick is to construct "before" and "after" essay questions that require the same primary skills in order to minimize the problem of the comparability of the essays.

Some people give "before" and "after" essays to outside readers for blind "matched pairs" comparisons, in which the readers read pairs and decide which of the two is better. Afterward, they check to see if, more often than not, a student's more recently written papers fared better than the early work; if so, he or she probably improved. Because this is a less reliable approach, it is usually employed along with some other kinds of evaluation.

(8) Research

Research is a luxury, of course, but it is an important consideration, and many school districts, community colleges, and universities have the resources for carrying on long-term research. Researchers will require various kinds of writing samples gathered under varying circumstances over long periods of time, for little sensible research can be carried out with standardized test scores alone. Long-term study—for example, of the nature of coherence problems and their solution or of successful strategies for ameliorating bidialectical interference problems—can benefit any institution both economically and educationally. This suggests that there should be an essay component to whatever test you settle upon.

(9) A Test That Teaches

Every test is a message to the test-taker. A poorly constructed multiple-choice test, for instance, might tell students that there are only four ways to fix an awkward sentence, one of which is ridiculous, one of which is highly implausible, and two of which differ in only trivial ways. Most multiple-choice tests tell students and teachers alike that the most important aspects of writing are capitalization, punctuation, spelling, and vocabulary—a dangerously misleading message to send to impressionable people. A poorly designed essay assignment can tell students that writing is "letting it all hang out," which is just as misleading. Assignments that ask for descriptive writing but are graded for grammar communicate the insidious message that teachers are devious.

It is often instructive to expose students to the process of essay evaluation. They can learn a great deal if they have to select particular writing skills to be tested, write unequivocal test directions, and establish specific criteria for successful performance. In the process of brainstorming assignments together, debating criteria for excellence, analyzing component skills, and grading papers, students internalize a systematic approach to writing that they can use in all writing situations.

(10) Everything

No one test will serve all of the purposes I have mentioned. However, an evaluation system can. Nothing can match the accuracy, fairness, and utility of a long-term, systematic, integrated evaluation system that combines a variety of tests with survey information, teacher observation, and research findings.

The Content of Tests

Now that you have considered the uses to which you will put your test, you must consider its content. Test content might well be dictated by a desire to assess any of the following:

Writing apprehension and anxiety	Knowledge of usage
Attitudes toward written language	Reasoning skills
	Expressiveness
Prewriting skills	Persuasiveness
List-making skills	Analytical ability
Outlining	Narrative skills
Composing strategies	Descriptive skills
Editing skills	Penmanship
Knowledge of grammar	Semantic maturity
Sentence-combining skills	Syntactic maturity
	Rewriting skills

I have heard everything on this list called "basic," but I know of no test that assesses more than a few of these important aspects of writing. The list serves primarily to dramatize the complexity of a comprehensive evaluation program—which would assess all of these things—compared with a test, which would measure only a few. Although space does not permit detailed discussion of each aspect, one thing that has not already been mentioned deserves attention.

There are "writing apprehension" instruments available. Some are surveys that ask direct questions ("Do you stall a lot before you start writing?"), and some are organized around various Likert-type scales ("I am (a) not (b) a little (c) quite (d) very nervous about my spelling"). They are relatively easy to create and usually worth creating. Even if actual writing progress is slow, it can be a source of satisfaction to a teacher to discover that he or she is improving attitudes toward writing.

Another content-related consideration is this: Do you want your test to relate to your specific curriculum or student population? What, exactly, are you teaching your students about writing? A test (purchased or created) that does not match a school's curriculum or student population's special needs is not a fair appraisal of abilities. No one will be able to truly interpret the results, and teachers will be unable to remedy problems suggested by the results. Nationally marketed commercial tests cannot match your curriculum exactly. Rather than changing your curriculum to match the test (a mistake, considering the limited coverage of such tests and the purposes for which they are intended), you should supplement the test with material more suitable to your curriculum and more relevant to the problems of your students. Only you know those problems; test developers can but guess.

There is a slight but important difference between what you are ostensibly teaching and what you are teaching in fact. All of us have blind spots and hidden prejudices about the kinds of writing we prefer. Students are as sensitive to our unintended as to our intended messages about writing. Careful analysis of your approach can eliminate any contradictions you may be communicating and eliminate, as well, the possibility that your students are giving you what you want even when you do not know it is what you want.

Purchasing or Creating Tests

One more set of questions ought to be answered before you decide which test to buy, which to create:

1. Does your school administration have a genuine commitment to the improvement of writing?

2. Is the evaluation of writing left only to the English department?
3. How much money and time do you have, how many students are involved, and what other resources (teaching aids, graduate assistants, lay readers, computers, research labs, etc.) do you have?

(1) Administrative Support

Experience has shown that the effectiveness of evaluation programs is related to the amount of administrative support they receive. Lukewarm support may be adequate reinforcement for a modest, cheap testing program but never for a full-scale, responsible evaluation. In some cases half-hearted support is worse than no support at all. Many administrators simply do not know very much about writing or its productive evaluation. It becomes the obligation, then, of the writing teacher to educate administrators to the complexity of the subject and the long-term cost effectiveness of responsible evaluation. Short-sighted, one-shot testing systems may well solve the immediate logistical problems of paramount concern to administrators, but they cannot, by themselves, assist either teachers or students. In the end the school that opts for such an approach loses more in the quality of its graduates than it gains in cost benefits accrued.

(2) Institution-wide Responsibility

Some two-year colleges, small four-year colleges, and even universities insist that the improvement of writing is a challenge to the entire institution, not just the English department. School-wide writing programs—such as those at Beaver College (Pennsylvania), Central College (Iowa), Gustavus Adolphus (Minnesota), and Carleton College (Minnesota)—are springing up like mushrooms. In some cases every faculty member receives intensive in-service training in writing theory and instruction. In others, every department is required to teach writing, but in its own way. In still others the English department carries the primary responsibility, but the other departments are required to refer students to writing laboratories for specific problems. This range, from comprehensive change to slight modification of the present system, spans a multitude of approaches that differ as the characters of the institutions and their resources differ. If your institution is headed in this direction, there are many consequences for the kind of test or evaluation program you will want to establish. The most obvious consequence will be that, in addition to all of the ingredients of an evaluation program already discussed, you will need to consider the nature of discourse in other content areas.

(3) Logistics

The answers to the logistical question become important factors in the equation anyone uses to choose an appropriate instrument or program. They are so interdependent that they cannot be discussed separately, and it is difficult to generalize about them. Obviously, if you are testing many students but have little money, you can subsample for scoring, stagger the testing over various budgets, depend upon colleagues for free assistance, use graduate assistants, or do any number of things to make ends meet. A teacher with few students can evaluate more aspects of writing than can a teacher with an equal amount of money but many more students. Each case will be somewhat different, and everyone will have to make at least some compromises.

Conclusion

If you extract from this essay the questions I have raised and answer each specifically, you should be in a better position to shop for or create a test that meets your needs. But it should be clear by now that I do not believe any *single* test is ever sufficient to answer the needs either of teachers or of their many audiences. I clearly favor an integrated evaluation system comprised of many different kinds of tests and based primarily upon the careful analysis of students and their actual, as opposed to inferred, writing. I believe that neither the ancient fear of "subjectivity" in essay evaluation nor the modern obsession with "correlations" is warranted any longer. Both extremes have done more to paralyze evaluation of writing than advance it. In the last two decades we have learned more than enough from evaluators, linguists, psychologists, rhetoricians, and ethnographers to keep us busy creating new evaluation systems for as long as we and our clients find it necessary.

IV Training Basic Writing Teachers

9 Training Teachers of Basic Writing

Constance J. Gefvert
Virginia Polytechnic Institute and State University

Gefvert emphasizes that the training of basic writing instructors should provide background in sociolinguistics and ESL methodology. The program of study she outlines could well serve as an in-service training course for instructors faced with teaching basic writing classes for the first time.

I recently submitted a proposal for a new graduate course in the English department at Virginia Tech, entitled "Techniques of Teaching Basic Writing." The course proposal was approved by our graduate committee, department head, and the dean of the College of Arts and Sciences. The final step before the course could be offered was to get the approval of the dean of the Graduate School, who called me in to talk about the course proposal. I don't understand, said the dean, why you want to teach college teachers things like punctuation, handwriting, spelling, and vocabulary—if they don't know those things by now, they certainly shouldn't be teaching in college! I was, needless to say, taken aback, yet it was a fair question. Graduate deans, like traditionally trained English professors, are likely to perceive graduate study according to the traditional curriculum of the academy and are understandably suspicious that teaching basic skills is not a subject complex enough to teach in a graduate course.

I explained to the dean that the better a teacher is at using correct punctuation and spelling, the less apt he or she is to know how to teach it to the unskilled. I explained, too, that remedial or developmental courses are more difficult to teach than an average freshman writing class because basic writing students have special problems: some have perceptual problems and "learning disabilities"; some have problems with dialect interference that require the kind of skilled teaching long recognized as essential for teachers of English as a Second Language; and some are simply unskilled and unpracticed in the written code and need teachers who can help them best by teaching according to a "developmental" rather than a traditional "building blocks" model of composition.

In explaining all this to the dean, I pointed out that "handwriting" and "punctuation" and "spelling," as listed on the syllabus, represented some very complex knowledge about the language and ways to teach it. I showed him a copy of Shaughnessy's *Errors and Expectations* and pointed out that a press as traditionally conservative as Oxford had considered the subject both important enough and academically sophisticated enough to publish the book. Surely, if Oxford could publish a book about how to teach basic writing, we were justified in offering a graduate course in the area. The dean approved the course.

It is the purpose of this article to describe not only the course, but some of the specific methods that it teaches. Before I describe the course and methods, however, I think it worthwhile to comment on the justification for offering such a course, since questions like those raised by the dean are common among many English professors.

Rationale

A graduate course in the techniques of teaching basic writing skills is first of all justified by the market. Community colleges and open-admissions four-year institutions have an obvious need for teachers who are trained in the complexities of developmental language skills. Like the dean who approved the course, adminstrators responsible for curriculum and personnel are becoming increasingly aware that instructors need special kinds of training for teaching basic writing. A study by Sullins and Atwell points up some interesting data about what kind of preparation community college administrators look for in the instructors they hire to teach English.[1] The study surveyed one hundred community college administrators—presidents, deans, division directors, and others responsible for making personnel decisions—concerning what kind of preparation they looked for in the people they hired. Among education courses, these administrators placed high priority on developmental studies (basic and remedial skills). Among English courses those on which they placed the highest priority were courses in the teaching of composition and English language studies. Interestingly, the survey did not ask about courses in teaching remedial or basic English skills, probably because few or no English departments offer such courses.

Clearly, if it is desirable to offer training in developmental studies through education courses and to offer training in composition and language through English courses, then it is even more desirable to offer a course that brings together what is known about all three fields. In fact, a good teacher of basic writing skills does need to know something about all three—developmental theories of psychology, English language (especially the problem of dialect interference), and composition. The first time the new graduate course was taught, it included the latter of these two, but because of the tight schedule (a quarter system with only ten weeks), it touched on the first only indirectly. The model syllabus that I suggest later in this article, howver, is based on a semester of fifteen weeks and includes some of the materials that were not presented in the course.

The market, then, suggests one reason for training and retraining English teachers to deal specifically with problems of basic writing skills. It is obvious that employers want teachers who are both trained and experienced in these areas.[2] There is, however, a more theoretical justification for such training which has to do with the conditions under which students learn best. Our traditional approach to designing courses in basic writing is deductive: we assume certain skills need to be taught, and we proceed to teach these skills to all students in our basic writing classes, whether they need them or not. No wonder that students are often bored with such courses, resentful of the time they lose before getting into freshman English courses and disappointed that they really haven't learned much after all to help them gain the skills they lack. Instead, we need to design basic writing curricula inductively, based on the skills students lack and on what linguistics and developmental psychology can teach us about how students best learn these skills. It is important to train instructors, therefore, not only how to teach certain basic skills, but also how to discover what students need to learn, how to design courses and sequences that will teach those things, and how to design methods of individualized instruction in laboratories and other tutorial situations.[3] The emphasis on individualized instruction is especially important to insure that we meet the specific needs of each student without requiring all students to cover the entire sequence of materials if they need not.

Shaughnessy's *Errors and Expectations* is a model of inductive research concerning the kinds of errors students make as well as the patterns behind those errors, the reasons students make them, and how the errors are related developmentally to other errors or lack of skills. One of her conclusions is that there is no one way to teach all basic writers. Not only is each class comprised of students with a wide variety of problems, but the extent and kinds of problems also vary from class to class and from college to college. Her book, she says,

> assumes that programs are not the answers to the learning problems of students but that teachers are and that, indeed, good teachers

create good programs, that the best programs are developed *in situ*, in response to the needs of individual student populations and as reflections of the particular histories and resources of individual colleges.[4]

A study by Higgins likewise emphasizes the need for designing curricula based on descriptions of student writing. His study of the problems of basic writing students at York College, CUNY, and evaluation of basic writing text-workbooks concludes that "what the student requires in writing skills instruction is quite different from what these workbooks stress."[5] Because I too believe that teachers, rather than programs or textbooks, are the answers to the problems of basic writing students and that curricula and textbooks must be developed inductively, I also believe strongly that teachers must have the kind of training that will enable them to make the necessary individual decisions about what is appropriate for certain students in certain situations. They must have enough knowledge, both theoretical and practical, to be able to adapt to each student and not to be dependent either on a course syllabus or on a certain textbook.

A good illustration of how important it is to develop curricula inductively is a study done by Moment.[6] She compared the writing of students in a basic writing course with that of students in the first quarter of a freshman English sequence at Virginia Tech. She discovered that the variables listed below were the most significant in discriminating between the writing of the two groups.[7] The variables are listed in order of their ability to discriminate between students in these two courses and include not only errors but also certain rhetorical skills and certain measures of syntactic maturity included in her study.

1. Omission and duplication (perceptual errors)
2. Verb form (nonstandard forms of past and past participle as well as omission or nonstandard use of *-s* and *-ed* inflections)
3. Wording (confusion of words or incorrect use)
4. Shift in person
5. Comma errors
6. Development
7. Organization
8. Words per clause
9. Total words in a piece of writing
10. Diction (rhetorical effectiveness)
11. Words per T-unit
12. Pronoun reference
13. Clauses per T-unit

A number of observations can be made from this list. The kinds of sentence errors included in many textbooks for "remedial" or basic writing students do not appear on the list, although they were part of

Moment's study; and certain punctuation errors do not appear that are normally covered in basic writing texts (e.g., fragments, detached clauses and phrases, punctuation of restrictive modifiers). Since we have been teaching how to correct these kinds of errors in our basic writing course, we have either been spinning our wheels, teaching concepts the students already know, or we have been teaching concepts that are ordinarily taught in the regular freshman English sequence. The deductive manner in which we, and, I would venture to say, most other departments, have designed basic writing curricula has resulted in teaching concepts that our students do not need and ignoring those that they do. According to the above list, for example, we should be spending less time teaching students how to avoid fragments and more time on verb forms, commas, pronoun reference, and vocabulary. In the rhetorical area we need to spend more time on the basic skills of development, organization, and choosing diction appropriate to the audience. In the area of syntactic maturity, we should be doing much more with sentence combining, since research indicates that sentence combining does indeed increase syntactic maturity (defined by Mellon and Hunt in such terms as words per T-unit and clauses per T-unit).[8] Finally, since the first-place discriminator is omission and duplication, we need to be aware of students who have reading and perceptual problems, and possible learning disabilities as well.

Such a study as Moment's is evidence that we need to teach teachers how to diagnose their own students' learning difficulties, how to design courses inductively, and how to work individually with students in a laboratory situation. Moment's study and those previously mentioned present clear evidence and justification for a formal training program for teachers who will be instructing basic writing students. The course I am about to describe and some of the methods we have tried are examples of how a graduate department might go about designing training programs, whether as graduate courses or as in-service training.

Materials

Textbooks and other materials appropriate for a course in teaching basic writing skills are not plentiful. A number of books dealing with developmental students and developmental programs are available, but while they offer valuable background, they do not treat specifically the teaching of basic writing.[9] Some articles on teaching basic writing have been published in professional journals, and are being published in increasing numbers; unfortunately, these are too often merely anecdotal, describing programs that have worked successfully in particular colleges or universities and are seldom based on data gathered from inductive studies of the students the programs are meant to serve.

Only recently have we been fortunate enough to have published materials readily available that deal with various aspects of teaching basic writing and that are based firmly on research and verifiable data. The most comprehensive, most scholarly, and most readable of all such materials is Shaughnessy's *Errors and Expectations*. As will be apparent from the description of the course, we depended heavily on this book, both for data to give us a picture of basic writing students and for suggestions about how to teach students with certain kinds of problems. One advantage of Shaughnessy's book is that the suggestions for teaching to specific problems are adaptable to different kinds of students in a variety of situations. Her book is based not on a single program that must be followed, but rather on a series of observations about basic writing students at CUNY and ways of dealing with individual problems. Her book thus lends itself to designing inductively courses that will fit the needs of certain students at certain institutions and to working with students individually, on a tutorial basis or in a laboratory.

Because Shaughnessy's book was the mainstay of the course, we organized the class sessions roughly according to the order of topics as she treats them, supplementing them with other books and articles. We used the volumes so far published of the new *Journal of Basic Writing*, as well as articles from other journals. Individual members of the class used other materials in their own research projects, many of which I have included in my model syllabus under "Resources." These included the collection of essays edited by Fasold and Shuy called *Teaching Standard English in the Inner City* and a collection of articles about teaching the basics published by NCTE as part of the *Classroom Practices* series.[10]

Finally, we used two textbooks for basic writing students as resources for developing further materials; these were Strong's *Sentence Combining* and Gefvert, Raspa, and Richards' *Keys to American English*. Students in the class also consulted many other basic writing textbooks both in preparation for class discussion and for research papers, but we used these two with the whole class because they are aimed at accomplishing very specific goals for specific kinds of student problems—*Sentence Combining* for increasing syntactic maturity and *Keys to American English* for teaching standard English as a second dialect, using quasi-foreign language teaching techniques.

Course Design

I taught the course with the help of other faculty who had expertise in certain areas and occasionally presented a class session and with the help of the coordinator of our Writing Center and various tutors, who were responsible for the practicum part of the course. We held ten class meetings of two hours each during the winter quarter in which we discussed readings, held role-playing sessions in which students simulated tutoring basic writing students, and held theme-evaluating sessions in which we practiced analyzing the problems of students with a wide variety of basic writing problems and discussed possible ways of helping them, using Shaughnessy's analysis of student writing as a touchstone. We also spent time talking about some basic matters of dialect interference, second-language interference, and learning disabilities. Finally, we explored some specific techniques and methods of dealing with two problem areas for basic writing students: sentence structure and grammatical inflections. The methods we practiced were sentence combining, recognition drills, and pattern practice (these are explained in more detail in the course description).

After the quarter was over, each student was assigned to a practicum during the spring quarter, doing a tutoring internship for three hours a week in our Writing Center under the guidance of an experienced tutor and with the supervision of the coordinator of the Writing Center. Students also wrote a research paper during the spring quarter; they were encouraged to do original, empirical research concerning our students or programs, those of the high schools or community colleges in which they taught, or the kinds of problems faced by the students they were working with in the Writing Center.

Students received three quarter hours of graduate credit in English for the course. They registered for two quarters, and their grades were deferred until the practicum and the research paper were completed. Evaluation consisted of approximately equal weighting of the students' active participation in the winter quarter class meetings, their evaluation by the Writing Center tutor with whom they worked during the spring, and my evaluation of their research paper.

Model Syllabus

As noted earlier, the ten-week quarter imposed some important limitations on the content of the course. The model syllabus that follows is based on a fifteen-week semester, which is probably the norm for most universities that might offer such a course. Those on a quarter system would have to make allowances for the shorter time, whereas on a semester system, many schools might find it difficult to defer credit for a semester while the practicum is completed. It would be possible to run the practicum concurrently with the regular class meetings, particularly if the practicum did not begin until halfway through the semester, when students would have some theoretical background for teaching basic writing students and some experience with theme evaluation and role-playing tutoring. The syllabus that follows is concerned only with the classroom part of the course, not with the practicum.

General Format

Students should prepare for each class session in three ways. First, of course, they should read the assigned materials. Students are encouraged but not required to read the books listed under "Resources." These books should provide suggestions and materials for research papers. Second, in the texts that the graduate students are using for their own teaching or in other texts written for remedial-basic writing, they should look for and evaluate teaching techniques and exercises aimed at solving the problems discussed by Shaughnessy. (Are they effective in solving the problems they say they are intended to solve? Is there evidence of linguistic naïveté, lack of understanding of dialect-related problems, etc.? Are the exercises aimed only at correcting, or at composing as well? Are they apt to help students transfer what they learn from the textbook to their own writing?). These text evaluations will be used as the basis for discussion each week. Third, students should bring samples of writing from their own students (or, if they are not in-service teachers, from other students) that illustrate the principles, errors, or rhetorical problems being discussed each week. These writing samples should be duplicated and distributed to each class member at each class meeting and used as the basis for discussion.

The three activities outlined above provide the format for most class sessions. The remainder of this article presents the readings for each week, followed by a commentary on each class session.

Week 1: Introduction to the Course, Texts, and Syllabus

Reading. Shaughnessy, Mina. "Basic Writing." In *Teaching Composition: Ten Bibliographical Essays,* pp. 137-67. Ed. Gary Tate. Fort Worth: Texas Christian University, 1976.

Resource. Roueche, John E., and Jerry J. Snow. *Overcoming Learning Problems.* San Francisco: Jossey-Bass, 1977.

Commentary. In addition to the introduction to the course, which is a straightforward overview and explanation of the requirements and class format, two substantive topics are covered: the state of basic writing theory, pedagogy, and bibliography and "testing the waters" of essay evaluation. The lecture on the state of basic writing theory, pedagogy, and bibliography centers on Shaughnessy's bibliographic essay in Tate's collection, which describes both the dearth of research in basic writing and the contributions of linguistics and psychology—especially sociolinguistics (dialect variation), psycholinguistics (language acquisition and the connection between writing and reading skills), developmental psychology, evaluation techniques, and ESL theory and practice.

"Testing the waters" gives students a first opportunity to share evaluation of essays with their colleagues in the class. Here the instructor gives class members some papers from basic writing students and asks them to diagnose the problems of those students as displayed in their papers and to suggest ways of helping them. This activity should have several results. First, students should become aware of how differently they and their colleagues evaluate papers and how important it is to find some common ground. Second, they should realize how little they know about methods for dealing with basic writing problems and recognize the need for more objective data about basic writing skills. Third, they should understand how different each student is from every other student in a basic writing class and how necessary it is to design curricula inductively and individually.

Week 2: Attitudes Toward Students, Remediation, and Open-Door Colleges

Readings. (1) Shaughnessy, Mina. *Errors and Expectations: A Guide for the Teacher of Basic Writing.* New York: Oxford University Press, 1977, chapter 1. (2) Chaikas, Elaine. "Who Can Be Taught?" *College English* 35 (1974): 574-583. (3) Farrell, Thomas J. "Open Admissions, Orality, and Literacy." *Journal of Youth and Adolescence* 3 (1974): 247-260. (4) Finn, J. D. "Expectations and the Educational Environment." *Journal of Educational Research* 48 (1972): 387-410. (5) Griffin, Jacqueline. "Remedial Composition at an Open Door College." *College Composition and Communication* 20 (1967): 360-363. (6) Higgins, John C. "Remedial Students' Needs Versus Emphasis in Text-Workbooks." *College Composition and Communication* 24 (1973): 188-192. (7) Johnson, Paula, and Judith D. Hackman. "The Yale Average: or, After Competence, What?" *College Composition and Communication* 28 (1977): 227-231. (8) Lunsford, Andrea. "What We Know and Don't Know About Remedial Writing." *College Composition and Communication* 29 (1978): 47-52. (9) Shaughnessy, Mina. "Diving In: An Introduction to Basic Writing." *College Composition and Communication* 27 (1976): 234-239.

Commentary. The readings in this section emphasize a number of ideas. First, teachers need to have confidence in their students' ability to learn; they need to be aware that their students are not stupid or unable to learn—that, as Shaughnessy puts it,

> basic writing students write the way they do, not because they are slow or non-verbal, indifferent to or incapable of academic excellence, but because they are beginners and must, like all beginners, learn by making mistakes.[11]

Second, teachers need to understand some of the implications of open-door colleges and the kinds of students and student needs they confront in basic writing classes. Shaughnessy's journal article "Diving In" is the best description in print of the change in attitudes many teachers must undergo if they are to teach successfully the nontraditional student.

Discussion of student essays and textbooks this week focuses on reaction to and attitudes toward student papers—how to overcome the feeling of despair that "there's nothing I can do" or "this student is hopeless"; and on the attitude and tone of textbooks and how they potentially affect student performance.

Week 3: Attitude Toward Dialects—The Philosophy of Error

Readings. (1) Shaughnessy, Mina. *Errors and Expectations*, chapter 1. (2) D'Eloia, Sarah. "Teaching Standard Written English." *Journal of Basic Writing* 1 (1975): 5-13. (3) Halsted, Isabella. "Putting Error in Its Place." *Journal of Basic Writing* 1 (1975): 72-86. (4) Sledd, James. "Bidialectalism: The Linguistics of White Supremacy." *English Journal* 58 (1969): 1311-1317.

Resource. "Students' Right to Their Own Language." *College Composition and Communication.* Special Issue, 25 (Fall, 1974).

Commentary. These readings center on the problem of what "error" means, to what extent teachers should be concerned with it, and the difference between "error" on the one hand and dialect interference on the other. D'Eloia and Shaughnessy argue the importance of accepting that there is such a thing as error, a point of view Sledd implicitly rejects in his belief that teaching standard English as a second dialect is only another means of asserting "white supremacy" since standard English, according to Sledd, is the language of the white ruling class. Shaughnessy is concerned about the practical implications of her students' learning standard English and, in contrast to Sledd, is less concerned about the theoretical political implications. She voices my own view better than I could when she points out, first, that there is not such a neat system of dialect variation as some linguists would like to believe; second, that students themselves desire to control the language rather than let it control them; and, finally, that the "economics of energy" makes it necessary in a literate society to use the dominant code so that readers are conscious of the meaning that the code conveys, not of the code itself.[12] Both Shaughnessy's book and this course are founded on those three beliefs, together with the assumption that the "students' right to their own language" must be balanced by their right to the dominant code of a literate society.

Essay and textbook evaluation in this session focus on the philosophy of error displayed by class members in evaluating essays and by authors of textbooks.

Week 4: Handwriting and Punctuation

Reading. Shaughnessy, Mina. *Errors and Expectations,* chapter 2.

Commentary. Shaughnessy explains that handwriting and punctuation problems of basic writing students stem at least in part from their unfamiliarity with the written code. She discusses the purpose of punctuation—to be a map to guide the reader[13]—and ways of teaching punctuation through both analysis of sentence structure (basic writing students depend too much on the "ear" they have developed in a largely oral culture) and through sentence combining.[14] Her suggested exercises for both methods of teaching punctuation are discussed during this week, but a great deal more time is devoted to the relationship between syntax and punctuation during weeks six and seven.

Student papers are evaluated specifically for problems with handwriting and punctuation, and textbooks are evaluated according to how thoroughly and effectively they treat these problems.

Week 5: Syntax

Reading. Shaughnessy, Mina. *Errors and Expectations,* chapter 3.

Resources. (1) D'Eloia, Sarah. "The Uses—and Limits—of Grammar." *Journal of Basic Writing* 3 (1977): 1-48. (2) Kunz, Linda Ann. "X-Word Grammar: Offspring of Sector Analysis." *Journal of Basic Writing* 3 (1977): 63-76. (3) Gray, Barbara Quint, and Alice Trillin. "Animating Grammar: Principles for the Development of Video-Tape Materials." *Journal of Basic Writing* 3 (1977): 77-91.

Commentary. The class concentrates on what Shaughnessy calls "the syntax of competence," rather than the "syntax of style" that is the focus in more advanced writing courses.[15] Shaughnessy catalogs sentence errors into accidental errors (indicating a need for proofreading), blurred errors that create a kind of "syntactic dissonance,"[16] "consolidation errors" (related to the traditional parallelism), and inversions, some related to the traditional category of pronoun reference errors and problems with the place-marker *it*. The cures she suggests include sentence combining (see week seven), pattern practice (see week six), and exposure to mature, adult syntax through reading.

Analysis of essays this week concentrates on the kinds of syntactical errors Shaughnessy describes; evaluation of textbooks is based on the thoroughness with which they describe and offer help for syntactical problems.

Week 6: An Approach to Teaching Syntax and Sentence Punctuation

Readings. (1) Feigenbaum, Irwin. "The Use of Nonstandard English in Teaching Standard English: Comparison and Contrast." In *Teaching Standard English in the Inner City*, pp. 87-104. Ed. Ralph W. Fasold and Roger W. Shuy. Washington, D. C.: Center for Applied Linguistics, 1970. (2) Stewart, William A. "Foreign Language Teaching Methods in Quasi-Foreign Language Situations," pp. 1-19. In *Teaching Standard English in the Inner City.*

Resources. (1) Gefvert, Constance, Richard Raspa, and Amy Richards. *Keys to American English.* New York: Harcourt Brace Jovanovich, 1975. (2) Howland, Larry, ed. *The Writing Laboratory Report and Handbook.* Vol. 1: *General Orientation.* Columbia, S. C.: University of South Carolina, 1977. (3) Bannow, Steve, ed. *The Writing Laboratory Report and Handbook.* Vol. 2: *Workshops.* Columbia, S. C.: University of South Carolina, 1977.

Commentary. This class session constitutes a workshop in teaching sentence structure for the purpose of creating syntactic fluency and teaching conventional punctuation. The readings for this week by Feigenbaum and Stewart give the theoretical background for adapting ESL techniques to the teaching of English as a second dialect. The description below follows these authors in adapting ESL methods to teach standard English sentence structure and punctuation to students who either speak different dialects or are unfamiliar with the written code.

Phrases. Phrases are explained as a group of words related to each other in one of several ways. They are defined by form rather than by function, since knowing the grammatical function of phrases is not usually necessary for using correct punctuation at the basic level:

1. Prepositional phrase = a preposition + a noun (or noun substitute) + any related words. (Prepositions constitute a closed class, and students can simply be shown a list of them to which they may refer, as a learner of a second language might, until the words become familiar and easily recognizable.)

2. Infinitive phrase = infinitive (*to* + base form of verb) + words that describe or complete it.
3. *-ing* phrase = a noun or adjective made from the *-ing* form of a verb + words that describe or complete it.
4. *-ed* phrase = a word made from a past participle + words that describe or complete it. (Here the symbol *-ed* is used to represent both regular *-ed* participles and irregular participles.)

Clauses. A clause is defined as a group of words (which may include phrases) that has a subject and complete verb. Students are given separate sets of identification drills for phrases, clauses, and distinguishing phrases and clauses. To further fix in their minds the difference between phrases and clauses, additional exercises are given for practice in converting phrases into clauses.

Sentences, conjunctions, and relative pronouns. Students are given the following definitions:

> Sentence = a structure with at least one independent clause.
>
> An independent clause = a clause that does not begin with either a dependent conjunction or a relative pronoun, or is not a reduction of a relative clause.

Like prepositions, conjunctions (both dependent and independent) and relative pronouns are a closed list. Students can be trained to recognize that if a structure has only clauses that begin with dependent conjunctions or relative pronouns, it is not a sentence. Students are given identification drills to distinguish between dependent and independent clauses, drills in combining single clauses into compound sentences, identification drills in recognizing relative clauses, and pattern practice for using relative pronouns.

Punctuation in phrases, clauses, and sentences. Students are taught which marks of punctuation are used with which kinds of clauses and sentences:

1. End punctuation = period, question mark, or exclamation mark (after a structure beginning with a capital letter).
2. Semi-colons are used between two independent clauses, the first beginning with a capital letter and the second with a small letter.
3. Commas are used between two independent clauses only if there is an independent conjunction before the second; otherwise, they are used only between words, phrases, dependent clauses, and dependent and independent clauses.

Students are given practice in distinguishing conventional punctuation from unconventional.

Punctuation errors. It is worth noting that fragments, comma splices, and run-on sentences, traditionally described in handbooks as sentence errors, are really punctuation errors that have to do with the conventions of the written code. While an analysis of sentence structure, even as simple as the one just described, will help students to punctuate, the errors themselves are the result of incorrect punctuation rather than garbled sentence structure. (This is easily demonstrated by having students read a sentence aloud, in which case the punctuation disappears and there is no question of fragment, comma splice, or run-on sentence.)

In the workshop to which this week's class session is devoted, approximately half the time is spent describing the above ways of teaching sentence punctuation. The other half is spent in a demonstration (by members of the Writing Center staff) of one-on-one tutoring techniques. Class members then simulate the tutoring of a student with the kinds of punctuation problems described above; this gives the person in the role of teacher the opportunity to improvise. To work well, there must be many of them, and teachers must be able to make them up on the spot. Students will also profit from making up some of their own to test their classmates.

Week 7: Using Sentence Combining to Teach Syntactic Fluency and Punctuation

Readings. (1) Combs, Warren E. "Further Effects of Sentence-Combining Practice on Writing Ability." *Research in the Teaching of English* 10 (1976): 137-149. (2) Cooper, Charles R. "An Outline for Writing Sentence-Combining Problems." *English Journal* 62 (1973): 96-102, 108. (3) Daiker, Donald, Andrew Kerek, and Max Morenberg. "Sentence Combining and Syntactic Maturity in Freshman English." *College Composition and Communication* 29 (1978): 36-41. (4) Hunt, Kellogg W. "A Synopsis of Clause-to-Sentence Length Factors." *English Journal* 54 (1965): 300, 305-309. (5) Hunt, Kellogg W. "Syntactic Maturity in School Children and Adults." *Monograph of the Society of Research in Child Development,* Vol. 31, No. 134 (1970).

Resources research. (1) Hunt, Kellogg W. *Grammatical Structures Written at Three Grade Levels.* Research Report No. 3. Champaign, Ill.: NCTE, 1965. (2) Hunt, Kellogg W. *Sentence Structures Used by Superior Students in Grades Four and Twelve, and by Superior Adults.* Project 5-0313, Cooperative Research Program, Office of Education, DHEW. Tallahassee: Florida State Univ., n.d. (3) Mellon, John C. *Transformational Sentence Combining: A Method for Enhancing the Development of Syntactic Fluency in English Composition.* Research Report

No. 10. Urbana, Ill.: NCTE, 1969. (4) O'Hare, Frank. *Sentence Combining: Improving Student Writing without Formal Grammar Instruction.* Research Report No. 15. Urbana, Ill.: NCTE, 1973. (5) Daiker, Donald, Andrew Kerek, and Max Morenberg. *Sentence Combining and the Teaching of Writing.* Akron, Ohio: University of Akron, 1979.

Resources (textbooks). (1) Daiker, Donald, Andrew Kerek, and Max Morenberg. *The Writer's Options: College Sentence Combining.* New York: Harper and Row, 1979. (2) Rippon, Michelle, and Walter E. Meyers. *Combining Sentences.* New York: Harcourt Brace Jovanovich, 1979. (3) Strong, William. *Sentence Combining: A Composing Book.* New York: Random House, 1973. (4) O'Hare, Frank. *Sentencecraft.* Lexington, Mass.: Ginn and Co., 1975.

Commentary. Sentence combining is used only marginally in the exercises for week six because it deserves a full class session of its own. Research done by Hunt, Mellon, and O'Hare[17] has proved that teaching students to combine simple kernel sentences into more complex sentences (through coordination, subordination, and "embedding") not only increases their syntactic fluency without formal grammatical analysis, but also teaches correct punctuation of sentences. The exercises, many examples of which can be found in Strong's *Sentence Combining* and its teacher's manual, are easily adaptable to any level of writing instruction, but they work particularly well with basic writers who have not learned the traditional grammatical terminology that would make an approach like the one described in week six more accessible. This week's class session is devoted to a number of activities: reviewing the research on sentence combining; practicing sentence combining through role-playing; and learning to write original sentence-combining exercises and to help students learn to write their own, with the help of the article by Cooper.

Week 8: An Approach to Teaching Common Errors

Readings. (1) Shaughnessy, Mina. *Errors and Expectations,* chapter 4. (2) Laurence, Patricia. "Error's Endless Train: Why Students Don't Perceive Errors." *Journal of Basic Writing* 1 (1975): 23-42. (3) Krishna, Valerie. "The Syntax of Error." *Journal of Basic Writing* 1 (1975): 43-49. (4) Davidson, David. "Sentence-Combining in an ESL Writing Program." *Journal of Basic Writing* 3 (1977): 42-62.

Resource. Keys to American English.

Commentary. In chapter 4 of *Errors and Expectations,* Shaughnessy treats a number of "common errors" that can be remedied by teaching discrete rules. While she includes errors of inflection, periphrasis, and time relationships, she gives greatest attention to inflection, examining both the causes of inflection errors (including dialect interference and hypercorrection) and how to deal with them. In this class session her analysis of common errors is discussed and compared with Laurence's and Krishna's. The class follows a workshop format to teach some ways of dealing with inflectional errors by presenting the standard English inflectional system as a second dialect to those whose native dialect differs from standard written English. (Class members should recall the articles by Feigenbaum and Stewart from week six.) The approach that follows is only illustrative of how to teach inflections bidialectally. The descriptions follow the method of *Keys to American English*.

Sample lesson 1: regular verbs, present time. The "base form" of the verb is its form before anything is added or changed. The inflection *-s* is added with *it, he, she,* or any singular noun; *-es* is added when the base ends in *ch, sh, x, z,* or *o.* Exercises give students practice in recognizing the standard English forms and distinguishing them from others; conversion and pattern drills allow active practice in using the newly taught forms.

When drills are used, it is essential that the three types—recognition, conversion, and pattern practice—be properly sequenced and that they be sufficient in number so that students not only learn the forms, but actually internalize them and become so familiar with them that they can use them spontaneously.[18] A thorough set of drills will include about eighty of each type; the set may be followed by a free-writing exercise in which the standard forms are to be used.

Sample lesson 2: regular verbs, past time. The past of regular verbs is formed by adding *-ed* to the base form or *-d* if the base ends in *e.* The final consonant of the base form is doubled before adding *-ed* in words of one syllable or in words of more than one syllable if all three of the following exist: the last syllable is stressed, the last syllable ends with a single consonant, and the preceding vowel is short *(begged, permitted).* In words ending in *y,* the *y* is changed to *i* before adding *-ed (tried, carried);* the exception is words ending in *y* preceded by a vowel *(play).*

Again, it is essential that the number of drill items be sufficient to enable the student to internalize and produce spontaneously the standard forms. Having students complete a dozen or so drill items may suffice for them to understand how the new forms are made, but it will not enable them to produce the new forms with the familiarity and confidence needed for writing and speaking. Students will not be able to succeed in composing fluid, coherent prose if they constantly stop during their writing to review rules for forming verbs.

Sample lesson 3: the verb be *in present time. Be* is the only irregular verb besides *have* that is irregular in the present as well as the past.

Students need to be given the paradigm for the present of *be* and then exercises in recognizing and using the standard forms. The verbs *have* and *do* should also be taught in separate lessons.

Sample lesson 4: other irregular verbs. This lesson begins with a summary of previous lessons on irregular verbs. Next, such verbs as *hit* and *burst* are presented: the present is formed like the regular verbs, but the past is the same as the base. The present of all other irregular verbs is formed like regular verbs; the past is formed by changing the spelling of the base form. Here a list of irregular past tense forms should be given; students will have to learn the forms as they would irregular verbs in a foreign language.

Sample lesson 5: regular noun plurals. The inflection *-s* is added to form regular noun plurals, with some exceptions. When a noun ends in *s, x, sh, ch,* and sometimes in *o,* the inflection *-es* is added. An *f* at the end of a noun is changed to *v* and followed by *-es.* A *y* at the end of a noun is changed to *i* and *-es* is added, except when the *y* is preceded by a vowel *(plays, days).*

Sample lesson 6: possessive nouns, singular. Students are shown how the language can indicate possession either by inflection *(-'s)* or by periphrasis *(of . . .).* These methods are distinguished from the method used in some dialects of showing possession by juxtaposition *(John shoes).*

Sample lesson 7: possessive pronouns. Students are shown two forms of the possessive pronoun, one that precedes a noun *(her book)* and one that substitutes for a noun *(It is hers* instead of *It is her book).* It is necessary to stress that while possessive nouns use an apostrophe, possessive pronouns never do.

During this class, students simulate tutorial sessions as well as class sessions. Like the workshop in week six, this one will encourage class members to create exercises of their own and later to encourage their students to create their own exercises.

Week 9: Spelling and Vocabulary

Readings. Shaughnessy, Mina. *Errors and Expectations,* chapters 5 and 6.

Commentary. Shaughnessy's chapters on spelling and vocabulary are so detailed that to do them justice, to practice suggested exercises and methods, and to evaluate essays and textbooks adequately would take several weeks. The purpose of this course, however, is to give students the tools they will need to be effective teachers of basic writing. Thus, some practice in class (role-playing is always the most effective) with evaluating student essays for spelling and vocabulary problems and creating ways of assisting students will help class members develop techniques to handle the problems they will encounter when confronted by real students. This class session emphasizes role-playing conferences, evaluating papers, and suggesting solutions to student problems, with time left for discussing class members' evaluations of textbooks in these areas.

Week 10: Composing

Readings. (1) Shaughnessy, Mina. *Errors and Expectations,* chapter 7. (2) Farrell, Thomas J. "Developing Literate Writing." *Journal of Basic Writing* 5 (1978): 30-51. (3) Holloway, Karla F. C. "Teaching Composition Through Outlining." In *Classroom Practices in Teaching English, 1977-78: Teaching the Basics—Really!,* pp. 36-39. Ed. Ouida Clapp. Urbana, Ill.: NCTE, 1977. (4) Lunsford, Andrea. "Let's Get Back to the Classics." *Journal of Basic Writing* 5 (1978): 2-12. (5) Lamberg, Walter J. "Following a Short Narrative Through the Composing Process." In *Classroom Practices, 1977-78,* pp. 30-35. (6) Samuels, Marilyn Schauer. "Norman Holland's 'New Paradigm' and the Teaching of Writing." *Journal of Basic Writing* 5 (1978): 52-61. (7) Shuman, R. Baird. "Basics in Composition: Fluency First." In *Classroom Practices, 1977-78,* pp. 43-46. (8) Smith, Susan Belasco. "A Workable Approach to Teaching Composition." In *Classroom Practices, 1977-78,* pp. 40-42. (9) Silver, Stanfill. "The Great American One-Sentence Summary." In *Classroom Practices, 1977-78,* pp. 47-49.

Commentary. Shaughnessy's chapter entitled "Beyond the Sentence" presents a broad overview of the problem basic writing students have in composing anything longer than a sentence and emphasizes that basic writing students need help in conceiving an audience beyond themselves, especially an academic audience. She offers specific strategies for helping students learn to do traditional kinds of academic writing, as do the authors of the other articles assigned for this week. The class session includes discussion of these various approaches, along with evaluation of essays and discussions of which methods would work best with each student. Again, role-playing in a mock-tutorial situation is very helpful. Textbooks should be evaluated for the effectiveness with which they attack the problems Shaughnessy describes, but they should also be examined for the emphasis they give to composition, to grammar, syntax, and common errors, and to matters like punctuation, spelling, and vocabulary. By this time in the term, class members should be weighing the relative value of each kind of problem and, in the context of the earlier discussions about the philosophy of error, be able to make judgments about how much weight should be given to different items in a basic writing curriculum, in preparation for the discussion in week fifteen.

Week 11: Teaching Reading

Readings. (1) Fitzgerald, Thomas P., and Phillip M. Connors. "Structuring Comprehension with Key Words." In *Classroom Practices in Teaching English, 1977-78: Teaching the Basics—Really!*, pp. 6-9. Ed. Ouida Clapp. Urbana, Ill.: NCTE, 1977. (2) Melamed, Evelyn B., and Harvey Minkoff. "Transitions: A Key to Mature Reading and Writing." In *Classroom Practices, 1977-78*, pp. 17-21. (3) Scales, Alice M., and Shirley A. Biggs. "College Reading and Study Skills: An Assessment-Prescriptive Model." In *Classroom Practices, 1977-78*, pp. 22-28. (4) Smith, Arthur E. "Three Elements of Critical Reading." In *Classroom Practices, 1977-78*, pp. 2-5. (5) Tomas, Douglas A., and Thomas Newkirk. "Filling in the Blanks: Using the Cloze Procedure for Teaching Basic Skills." In *Classroom Practices, 1977-78*, pp. 10-16.

Resources. (1) Goodman, Kenneth, ed. *Miscue Analysis: Applications to Reading Instruction.* Urbana, Ill.: NCTE and ERIC/RCS, 1973. (2) Yarington, David. *The Great American Reading Machine.* Rochelle Park, N. J.: Hayden, 1977.

Commentary. The teaching of reading is a complex subject, one that obviously cannot be covered adequately in a week. Class members should, however, gain some understanding of the relationship between reading and writing skills, be able to help students with reading problems at least until more intensive professional help can be obtained, know how and how much to incorporate reading into a writing curriculum, and know how and when to refer students to reading-study skills specialists. The class session is spent discussing these issues and role-playing student conferences. Student essays will be examined for evidence of reading problems, and textbooks will be evaluated according to their awareness of the relationship between reading and writing.

Week 12: Special Problems in Teaching English as a Second Language

Readings. (1) Lay, Nancy. "Chinese Language Interference in Written English." *Journal of Basic Writing* 1 (1975): 50-61. (2) Rizzo, Betty, and Santiago Villafane. "Spanish Influence on Written English." *Journal of Basic Writing* 1 (1975): 62-71. (3) Davidson, David M. "Sentence Combining in an ESL Writing Program." *Journal of Basic Writing* 3 (1975): 49-62.

Resources. (1) Frank, Marcella. *Modern English: Exercises for Non-*

Native Speakers. Part 1: Parts of Speech. Englewood Cliffs, N. J.: Prentice-Hall, 1972. (2) Frank, Marcella. *Modern English: Exercises for Non-Native Speakers. Part 2: Sentences and Complex Structures.* Englewood Cliffs, N. J.: Prentice-Hall, 1972. (3) Hirasawa, Louise, and Linda Markstein. *Developing Reading Skills: Advanced.* Rowley, Mass.: Newberry House, 1974. (4) Ross, Janet, and Gladys Doty. *Writing English: A Composition Text in English as a Foreign Language.* 2nd ed. New York: Harper and Row, 1975.

Commentary. Like reading, ESL is a specialized field, and basic writing students whose native language is not English should ideally be in an ESL class. Many times, however, especially in writing laboratory situations, it is not always possible to have an ESL instructor work with a foreign student. Furthermore, there are many marginal situations in which the English of native Americans has been influenced by a different native language of the parents or a combination of a foreign language and a nonstandard dialect of English (like the English spoken in Spanish Harlem, for example). For these reasons even a short introduction to some ESL teaching principles and materials will be helpful to students in the class. Class time this week is spent discussing the readings, evaluating essays written by students whose English is to some extent influenced by other languages, and evaluating textbooks that might be used to supplement regular basic writing texts.

Week 13: Special Considerations for Community College Programs

Readings. (1) Johnson, G. R. "Teacher Preparation for Community/Junior Colleges." *Community/Junior College Research Quarterly* 1 (1977): 249-256. (2) Pritchard, N. S. "The Training of the Junior College English Teacher." *College Composition and Communication* 21 (1970): 48-54.

Resources. (1) Arden, J. W., and W. A. Terrell. *Research and Development of English Programs in the Junior College.* Urbana, Ill.: NCTE, 1965. (2) Kasden, Lawrence. "Chairing a Two-Year College English Department." *ADE/MLA Bulletin,* September 1978, pp. 14-19.

Commentary. Because community colleges are the largest employer of specialists in basic writing, some time in this course needs to be spent on the special needs and characteristics of community college students, as well as on the practical matters of working with community college administrations, with laboratory programs, etc. A specialist in teaching writing in the community college should be invited to this class, with discussion centering on the ways in which the topics so far discussed in this course would be adapted to community colleges.

Week 14: Evaluation

Readings. (1) Shaughnessy, Mina. *Errors and Expectations*, chapter 8 and appendix. (2) Bernadette, Sr. Miriam. "Evaluation of Writing: A Three-Part Program." *English Journal* 54 (1965): 23-27. (3) Brown, Rexford. "What We Know Now and How We Could Know More about Writing Ability in America." *Journal of Basic Writing* 4 (1978): 1-6. (4) Cooper, Charles. "Measuring Growth in Writing." *English Journal* 64 (1975): 111-119. (5) Hake, Rosemary. "With No Apology: Teaching to the Test." *Journal of Basic Writing* 4 (1978): 39-62. (6) Harris, Muriel. "Evaluation: The Process for Revision." *Journal of Basic Writing* 4 (1978): 82-90. (7) Matthews, Roberta S. "The Evolution of One College's Attempt to Evaluate Student Writing." *Journal of Basic Writing* 4 (1978): 63-70. (8) McColly, William. "What Does Educational Research Say about the Judgment of Writing Ability?" *Journal of Educational Research* 64 (1970): 148-154. (9) McColly, William. "Composition Rating Scales for General Merit." *Journal of Educational Research* 59 (1965): 55-66. (10) McDonald, W. V. "Grading Student Writing: A Plea for Change." *College Composition and Communication* 26 (1975): 154-158. (11) Metzger, Elizabeth. "A Scheme for Measuring Growth in College Writing." *Journal of Basic Writing* 4 (1978): 71-81. (12) Noreen, R. G. "Placement Procedures for Freshman Composition." *College Composition and Communication* 28 (1977): 141-144. (13) Palmer, W. S. "Measuring Written Expression: Quality Scales and the Sentence." *High School Journal* 60 (1976): 32-40. (14) White, Edward M. "Mass Testing of Individual Writing: The California Model." *Journal of Basic Writing* 4 (1978): 18-38. (15) Williams, Joseph. "Re-evaluating Evaluating." *Journal of Basic Writing* 4 (1978): 7-17.

Resources. (1) Bloom, Benjamin, et al. *Handbook of Formative and Summative Evaluation of Student Learning.* New York: McGraw-Hill, 1971. (2) Braddock, Richard, et al. *Research in Written Composition.* Urbana, Ill.: NCTE, 1963. (3) California Association of Teachers of English. *A Scale of Evaluation of High School Student Essays.* Champaign, Ill.: NCTE, 1960. (4) Cooper, Charles, and Lee Odell, eds. *Evaluating Writing: Describing, Measuring, Judging.* Urbana, Ill.: NCTE, 1977. (5) Diederich, Paul B., et al. *Factors in Judgment of Writing Ability.* Princeton: Educational Testing Service, 1961. (6) Diederich, Paul B. *Measuring Growth in English.* Urbana, Ill.: NCTE, 1974. (7) Judine, Sr. M., ed. *A Guide for Evaluating Student Composition.* Urbana, Ill.: NCTE, 1965. (8) Larson, Richard L. "Selected Bibliography of Writing on the Evaluation of Students' Achievements in Composition." *Journal of Basic Writing* 4 (1978): 91-100.

Commentary. Evaluation is a technical subject that requires training in statistics and other areas about which English teachers are often ignorant. This class session should include a guest speaker who is a specialist in evaluation. The topics to be explored include ways in which professional evaluation experts can work with English teachers in diagnosis and placement, ways to evaluate student writing other than the traditional A-B-C-D-F manner, and ways to evaluate the effectiveness of basic writing classes.

Week 15: Designing Courses for Basic Writing Students

Readings. (1) Campbell, Dianna S., and Terry Ryan Meier. "A Design for a Developmental Writing Course for Academically Underprepared Black Students." *Journal of Basic Writing* 2 (1976): 20-30. (2) Desy, Jeanne. "Reasoned Writing for Basic Students: A Course Design." *Journal of Basic Writing* 2 (1976): 4-19. (3) Mills, Helen. "Language and Composition: Three Mastery Learning Courses in One Classroom." *Journal of Basic Writing* 2 (1976): 44-59. (4) Petrie, Anne. "Teaching the Thinking Process in Easy Writing." *Journal of Basic Writing* 2 (1976): 60-67. (5) Pierog, Paul. "Coaching Writing." *Journal of Basic Writing* 2 (1976): 68-77. (6) Ponsot, Marie. "Total Immersion." *Journal of Basic Writing* 2 (1976): 31-43.

Resources. (1) Mills, Helen. *Commanding Paragraphs.* Glenview, Ill.: Scott, Foresman, 1976. (2) Mills, Helen. *Commanding Sentences: A Charted Course in Basic Writing Skills.* Glenview, Ill.: Scott, Foresman, 1974.

Commentary. One of the fundamental assumptions underlying this course is that programs for basic writing students must be developed inductively rather than deductively in order to meet specific, individual needs rather than merely the generalized needs of a large group of students.

In this final session the class discusses the readings, all of which describe entire courses for basic writing students, and evaluates their potential usefulness or adaptability for students with different backgrounds and different needs. The class should also explore how to design a program, given limitations of budget and personnel, that best serves the largest number of students. The planning should include how to use a combination of classroom and laboratory to treat problems common to a large number of students while still leaving room for individual attention. A discussion of such practical matters is a fitting conclusion to a course that attempts to develop a special repertoire of techniques and a flexibility which will allow teachers of basic writing to teach effectively in whatever situation and within whatever constraints they may find themselves.

10 Staffing and Operating Peer-Tutoring Writing Centers

Kenneth A. Bruffee
Brooklyn College, CUNY

> Bruffee makes a case for the educational effectiveness of using peer tutors in basic writing centers. While his primary topic is the selection, training, and function of peer tutors, he also outlines important aspects of establishing and maintaining a writing center on campus.

Peer-tutoring writing centers are places where, in an informal setting, college students help other college students learn to write. In most peer-tutoring programs the tutors are trained, either in specially designed credit-bearing courses or in noncredit seminars. What follows is a general description of one such program, the Brooklyn College Writing Center, a peer-tutoring center which, since 1973, has served an average of 800 to 1,000 students each semester.[1] A similar program, adapted to conditions prevailing in two-year colleges, has been established at Nassau Community College.[2]

Purpose and Effectiveness

The main service performed by a peer-tutoring writing center for its college is to supplement formal classroom instruction in writing by offering an alternative, long-range context for learning. Students unquestionably learn a great deal about writing through formal instruction, and they need that instruction. But writing is not like riding a bike, which individuals learn once and never forget. It is something that students must learn and relearn as their education advances, as their ideas become more complex, and as they mature intellectually and emotionally. The purpose of a writing center is to help students develop their ability to write in ways tailored to their individual needs. Sometimes tutors work with students for several weeks, or even a semester or more.

In other cases tutors respond on an ad hoc basis, helping students cope with writing problems as they are asked to write papers and examinations in their subject-matter courses.

To be successful, therefore, a peer-tutoring program must have the proper educational context. It requires a campus where faculty recognize that writing is essential to learning. A writing center should be part of a campus-wide commitment to more and better student writing at all levels and in all fields. On the other hand, just as a peer-tutoring writing center requires campus commitment to writing, it can also be an effective tool for gaining that commitment. This is the second value a writing center may have for its college. An active, visible writing center which engages enthusiastic undergraduate peer tutors in its "intracurricular activity" of developing students' writing can draw attention to writing throughout the campus. Finally, peer tutoring has a hidden bonus that I will discuss at the end of this essay: it can bring to a college the important social dimension of learning that mass higher education sorely lacks.

The evidence of the positive effects of peer tutoring on the writing of college students is not yet formal or rigorous. But the evidence is overwhelming that peer tutoring in general has immense potential. In *Peer and Cross-Age Tutoring in the Schools*, to my mind the best short guide to all aspects of peer tutoring, Bloom says,

> In 90 percent of the studies [reported], tutees made significant progress in school achievement measures—largely in the areas of reading and language arts. Thus, it is evident that a great variety of tutoring programs are effective in producing significant learning gains by tutees.[3]

Bloom cautions, however, that the studies she discusses "tend to be the more carefully designed" ones and that others

> are unlikely to produce these results, especially when the tutoring process is not continued long enough, when the tutoring program and materials are poorly structured, or when the materials available are inappropriate to the needs of the tutee. However, if the minimum conditions for tutoring ... are satisfied, with few exceptions the tutees made clear gains in cognitive learning.[4]

Although Bloom's evidence is drawn from work done principally in elementary and secondary schools, it strongly suggests that when peer tutoring in the less formal setting of a college writing center is properly evaluated, it too will prove effective.[5]

The success of peer tutoring at Nassau Community College and Brooklyn College tends to support this view, although it has been measured so far only informally. At Nassau, Beck reports that "a poll of classroom teachers indicated as much improvement in writing of students tutored by peers as those tutored by faculty; several instructors noticed increased enthusiasm about writing in general in students of peer tutors." The Brooklyn College Writing Center gauges its success by the numbers of students which it regularly serves, by the satisfaction of the tutors who work there, and by sheer survival.

Location and Organization

Location is crucial to a successful writing center. A drop-in writing center must be where the students are. Its furnishings can be plain and modest. It needs to have little more by way of equipment than tables, chairs, a couple of typewriters, and books (some rhetorics and a dictionary—preferably chained to the floor). But it absolutely must be placed where it is highly visible and readily accessible: in a room off the student cafeteria, on the first floor of the student center, off the entrance to the library, etc. At Brooklyn, for example, the writing center is across from the library on the walk where almost every student passes on the way in and out of the college gate.

Inside, everything possible must be done to make it easy to ask for help. The organization should be kept simple so that students don't feel they're being lassoed by red tape the minute they walk in the door. Record-keeping should be minimal and done unobstrusively only after the main job of helping has been done. At the Brooklyn center, tutors keep a personal log describing their work and their problems as tutors and as writers. They also enter on a 4 × 6 card the academic classification of each student they help, the type of help requested, and what they did to meet the problem. They do not record the names of the students they help, so that students, who are often intimidated, self-conscious, and embarrassed, feel as little as possible the risk of exposure. Tutors often trade names with students they work with, of course, and some agree to meet regularly with a clientele which they work up on their own. A teacher who wants to be sure a student assigned to get help has actually got it can ask the student to get a written report from the tutor describing the work they did together.

Naturally, there are limitations to the services that peer tutors provide. Some of these are imposed by the faculty and some by the tutors themselves. Peer tutors are not editors or ghost writers. Tutors soon realize that they have their own work to do and don't have time to do other students' work, too. With encouragement and practice, they get very good at saying no. Although many students need help with grammar, usage, and mechanics, the kind of help most students ask for is the kind peer tutors are most able to give: help in getting started and in discovering, expressing, and organizing ideas. Teachers and tutors together can make their own work sheets to use in tutoring or draw on textbook exercises relevant to the needs of the center's clientele.

Staff and Budget

A member of the English department faculty (or better still, several members part-time) should be assigned to a peer-tutoring center to answer tutors' questions and if necessary supplement their instruction—in effect, to tutor the tutors. Tutors may turn to the faculty member on duty or to each other for help at any time. This is one of the most important conditions under which peer tutors work in a center of this kind: they work independently as tutors, they are not closely monitored or "supervised," yet they always have access to help. Furthermore, when a tutor turns to a dictionary, a rhetoric, or an instructor for help, tutees learn something fundamental to education: ignorance is nothing to be embarrassed about; it is not equivalent to stupidity. To admit that you don't know something is the essential first step to learning.

Because a peer-tutoring center deals with such basic attitudes toward learning, and because it is central to a campus-wide concern for writing, it should be funded by the college as a whole. Also, because a peer-tutoring program differs structurally from more conventional tutoring programs, it may require some innovative budgeting. In conventional tutoring programs, faculty or graduate assistants work directly with undergraduates. The budget for these programs covers the wages of those directly involved. In contrast, a peer-tutoring program lessens these costs because fewer staff members work directly with students. Instead, the staff teaches writing indirectly through a cadre of trained undergraduates.

But a peer-tutoring program requires support of another kind. It has to pay faculty to supervise and teach tutors. An essential feature of the Brooklyn program, for example, is the writing course that prepares the tutors. By improving the tutors' own writing through a process of peer criticism, these courses keep the level of tutoring high and maintain the tutors' awareness of the difficulties writers face. In addition, the courses insure a continual supply of capable peer tutors sufficient to meet the needs of the college. Sound, serious, credit-bearing writing courses to prepare tutors academically and support them in their work are as much a part of a peer-tutoring program as tutoring itself, since the best tutors are tutors who write well themselves.

One intermediate composition course is enough for most small writing center programs. Larger programs, and those (like the Brooklyn

College program) which sometimes supply trained and experienced big-brother and big-sister tutors to local high school writing programs, may add one or two more courses in order to increase the sophistication of selected, advanced peer tutors. One of these courses may be advanced composition. Another may be an elementary, practical course in the English language: semantics, grammar, and linguistics. Instructors who teach these courses, furthermore, require special expertise. They should teach as much as possible through techniques of group inquiry and collaborative learning in order to engage tutors actively in learning, just as they in turn actively engage those they tutor.

Most programs which do not train tutors in credit-bearing courses nevertheless provide training of some kind. Tutors work in small groups with a supervisor, meet for informal sessions to discuss specific problems, observe themselves tutoring through closed-circuit television, and so on. Most programs also train tutors to some degree in teaching techniques.[6]

It would seem normal in terms of the division of academic labor for writing tutors to be trained by members of the English department. At the same time it is unfair to make a writing center the exclusive budgetary burden of the English department. Courses for peer tutors can put undue strain on the resources of the department that offers them, because enrollment in writing courses at every level must be kept relatively low and tutor training requires a closer than usual relationship between the undergraduates and the person training them. Moreover, the college as a whole, not just one or two departments, benefits directly and positively from these courses.

A peer-tutoring writing center should therefore be funded in a special way. Funds for the writing center should be added regularly to the budget of the department or unit assigned to teach the tutors. These funds should be stipulated to cover, first, the necessary courses given as part of the regular curriculum and, second, the wages of the faculty who work as resource personnel in the center itself. Finally, some allowance should be made to pay a few advanced tutors; since tutoring is itself part of the requirement of the first semester of preparation, tutors are not paid until that credit-bearing semester has been completed.

Selecting Tutors

Normally, tutors can be selected through teachers of freshman composition or in some cases through more advanced courses in a variety of disciplines. A letter of invitation describing the course, the work involved, and the advantages of being a tutor may be sent to students recommended in this way. In response to such an invitation, a kind of self-selection normally occurs. Those the idea appeals to gravitate toward the program; those put off by it do not respond. In addition, in some colleges the writing center faculty may interview prospective tutors. It is difficult at best, however, to identify potentially good tutors and eliminate potentially weak ones from a given group of fairly competent students. Experience seems to suggest that interviewing may be helpful, but may also be more time-consuming than it is worth.

The invitation itself is the key to successful recruitment. The letter describing the Brooklyn program, for example, emphasizes the characteristics which tend to make good tutors. The best tutors are relatively mature, capable of working well with other people, and interested in helping their fellow students. They must of course be competent writers. But for this work, human qualities are as important as academic excellence. Besides describing the course requirements (log, papers, peer critiques, tutoring three hours or so a week) and the reward in credit hours, the invitation should also explain what a student may expect to get out of peer tutoring educationally and personally.

Peer tutors can generally expect to gain improved writing ability, closer ties with members of the faculty, better understanding of the purposes and aims of higher education, some degree of heightened self-awareness, and the satisfaction of being of direct and important service to their own student community and the college as a whole. At large colleges and universities, and especially at commuter schools like Brooklyn College, the expectation of a lessened sense of social and intellectual alienation through membership in the sort of tight-knit academic community that peer tutoring provides is itself tremendously appealing to many mature and competent students.

Ability to write well is an important but not necessarily primary qualification for peer tutors, because a peer-tutoring program assumes that writing is a process of human communication and that many students' writing problems are caused by the students' inability to imagine an intelligent, sympathetic audience.[7] For many student writers this state of mind proves to be an almost insuperable barrier to written expression and thus to mature thought and mental growth. Peer tutors who are personally sympathetic as well as academically competent can help their fellow undergraduates overcome that barrier.

Training Tutors

The intermediate writing course in which peer tutors at Brooklyn are prepared for their work has several unusual and perhaps unique characteristics. The semester is divided roughly in two.[8] During the first half the tutors concentrate mainly on writing, reviewing grammar, and learning techniques of analysis and evaluation. Their first two papers are written on topics of their own choice or on topics drawn from their subject-matter courses. The papers are organized in a simple, standard rhetorical form. During this period the tutors also begin tutoring more or less cold turkey. Until they have had some experience, tutors find discussions of tutoring too theoretical, and they are too apprehensive for anything more than general instructions to have much effect. Experienced tutors look after the beginners during these first few weeks, and the teacher devotes a few class hours to the problems of getting started as a tutor.

In the second half of the semester (roughly), the tutors write two more papers, this time on topics related to their tutoring. Class discussion now begins to concentrate less on writing per se, turning instead to issues and problems arising out of the tutoring experience. In addition to writing four papers during the term, tutors keep personal logs reflecting class discussion, their experience writing, and especially their experiences and problems tutoring. Occasionally, tutors read excerpts from their logs aloud in class as a basis for class discussion, and twice during the term the teacher reads the logs and comments on them to encourage informal reflection.

The work most crucial to preparing effective undergraduate peer tutors, however, is peer criticism. Every paper that tutors write for this course is read aloud to the class by its author and then receives careful criticism written by other tutors, in addition to the comments and evaluation of the teacher. The teacher also comments on and evaluates these written critiques. What appears at first, then, to be a light load of writing—four papers during a semester—turns out to be a relatively heavy load of four papers, eight critiques, and, toward the end of the semester, two responses by each author to critiques other tutors have written. This process of peer criticism is the classroom counterpart of the work tutors do in the writing center when they help other students improve their writing.

The process of peer criticism is progressive. The first set of critiques asks tutors to describe the papers rhetorically, and specifically *not* to evaluate them. Here tutors learn the difference between what a unit of prose "says" and what it "does"—the rhetorical purpose it serves in the essay.[9] In criticizing the second set of papers, tutors add to the rhetorical description a tactful, detailed evaluation telling authors what they did right as well as how they could improve their papers. Since the third and fourth papers are on topics the whole class is familiar with—the tutoring process itself—in writing peer critiques for these two papers, tutors are asked to take issue with content and argument as well as technique. Finally, authors are asked to comment on and reply to criticism, and critics are asked to evaluate each other's critical technique and manner.

Hence, the tutors learn through this progressive process of peer criticism to distinguish three types of analytical reading: objective, rhetorically descriptive analysis; evaluative or judgmental response; and reaction to the issues and point of view developed in a paper. To formal peer criticism of writing, the final set of critiques adds the formal peer evaluation of peer criticism itself. Tutors examine and evaluate the critical dialogue they have engaged in.[10]

The final grade in the course is based on all of the students' writing, including their peer critiques, and on the writing center staff's judgment of the way students have fulfilled their responsibilities as tutors. Since students write some of their assignments (the peer critiques) on writing which their classmates have done, punctuality in meeting deadlines is important in this course. Just as peer critiques are the classroom counterpart of tutoring, this necessary punctuality is the counterpart of the reliability that students must exercise as tutors.

Although some faculty work well instinctively with a procedure such as the one described here, others may find it useful to sharpen their awareness and acquire some new pedagogical tools before undertaking it. At Brooklyn College, faculty who intend to teach this course apprentice themselves to those who have experience teaching it by sitting in on the class and working in the writing center for a term. Perhaps the best way for instructors to develop most of the skill and attitudes appropriate to teaching the course would be to "take" the course themselves under specially designed workshop conditions.[11]

Educational Significance

This description of the training that tutors undergo and my earlier comments on the academic community that tutors enjoy in a peer-tutoring program should suggest that besides performing a valuable service for its college, a peer-tutoring writing center program also provides an important educational experience for the tutors. In fact, peer tutoring provides what educational sociologists call "the essential conditions for mobilizing peer-group influence around intellectual concerns."[12] In a context of socially productive, service-oriented social exchange, and as part of the credit-bearing curriculum, a peer-tutoring program develops in the tutors two inextricably related functions of the educated mind: evaluative judgment and verbal thought and expression.

Peer tutoring tends to help tutors learn better how to learn by bringing to bear, through peer tutoring and its classroom equivalent, peer criticism, the social and emotional foundation upon which intellectual work rests. As peer tutors and peer critics, students in the program face ideas as fluid, growing forces in their own minds and those of their peers, not as artificial entities fully formed in an abstract state. And they confront the personal and proprietary interest that people feel for their own ideas. In this way, they become much more aware than most students ever do of the fragility and uncertainty—and the inherent excitement and pleasure—of mental work. Peer tutoring therefore attacks the "writing crisis" at its root, which is not lack of "skills," but students' inability to recognize, formulate, and express ideas of their own and to integrate education into everyday social, emotional, and practical life.

V Research Opportunities and Resources

11 Research in Writing: The Issues

E. Donald Hirsch, Jr.
University of Virginia

> Hirsch asserts that basic writing is one of the few areas in English which is not only wide open for the serious researchers, but is also begging for their assistance. The essay serves to direct us toward specific areas, to define the needs, and to suggest the urgency for reliable as well as imaginative research.

Our field of composition is in a paradoxical situation. We enjoy greater prestige than we had a decade ago; we can now get jobs while other English teachers cannot; we know more than we used to know about techniques of teaching; and while we know that we must still conquer a huge, still unknown realm of learning, we also believe that this great domain *can* be explored successfully. We know also that there is room on this new frontier for any energetic spirit who wants to push back the boundaries of knowledge. Composition research is probably the most significant intellectual frontier in college English departments today. But the paradox arises from the other side of our work—our continuing uncertainty about basic facts and methods and, most wearisome of all, our unending task of reading papers and commenting on papers and ultimately grading papers.

There is no great breakthrough in sight to change this aspect of composition teaching, and we are rightly suspicious of schemes which claim to remove either drudgery from the teacher or hard work from our students. The rewards of our work can be great for student and teacher alike, and its importance is unrivalled. But for all this, the drudgery does remain, and it always will. So, when I speak of new research in composition, I don't foresee any ultimate change in the basic need for paper-reading by teachers and paper-writing by students. The research issues that I shall discuss concern improvements that can make this basic pattern yield better results.

In the topics that I will be touching on, the reader will detect my conviction that such improvements are connected with the problem of gaining a *consensus* among ourselves, unlikely as that may appear, in view of the diverse approaches, habits, and convictions that we have. Nonetheless, I believe that a future consensus among composition teachers is a feasible aim with regard to many issues which have divided us in the past. The reason I think so is that controversy over a subject always tends to diminish as knowledge about it gets broader and deeper.

The phenomenon is well known to historians of learning and is even acknowledged by Thomas Kuhn, despite his skeptical views associated with the word *paradigm*. (I'm referring of course to Kuhn's book *The Structure of Scientific Revolutions* [Chicago: University of Chicago Press, 1970].) He and his fellow intellectual and social historians agree that a subject of inquiry like composition experiences two principal stages in its growth as a discipline. The first stage, which Kuhn calls "immature," is a period when "a number of schools compete for the domination of a given field." This period is marked by controversies like our own, in which people "confronting the same phenomena describe and interpret them in different ways." With the gradual advance of knowledge, the conflicts subside, and a consensus builds up which forms the discipline into a genuine intellectual community. Members of this community can then take the foundations of their field for granted and can therefore direct their attention to the problems and subproblems to be solved. The community can also agree among themselves whether a particular piece of work does in fact constitute a genuine solution to a problem. At this more advanced period, progress in the discipline becomes rapid and exciting, and it is then that it first becomes a genuine or mature discipline. Where before progress had been sporadic, uncertain, and disputed, now each new piece of work can be assimilated and integrated with the rest so that the frontiers of the discipline are pushed back in a clearly understood way. While we would all agree that composition research has not reached this stage of maturity, there are good grounds for believing that it can do so before many more years elapse.

A Thought-Experiment

To suggest why my optimism is reasonable, I am going to perform what psychologists used to call a thought-experiment. I am going to suppose we really do possess some detailed and reliable knowledge that we actually don't possess right now, but which we could in fact uncover in a very few years. First, I'm going to assume in my thought-experiment that we have found out some reliable facts about how long it normally takes to make a discernible improvement in certain subskills of writing for students between the ages of sixteen and twenty-five. And the point of my thought-experiment will be to illustrate how such an increase in our empirical knowledge will tend to create a consensus among us, where before there existed among us a great deal of pseudo-empirical, ideological, or what might be called theological debate.

Psychologists have recently made rather precise a concept about skill acquisition which we all know intuitively and which has long existed in memory theory as a contrast between passive recognition and active recall. Another version of this psychological contrast is expressed in our own discipline as the contrast between a passive vocabulary and an active vocabulary. It's well known that we passively understand many more words than we actively use. Yet, given world enough and time, we can dredge up from our passive vocabularies a number of words that we don't habitually use in ordinary speech and writing. Some of these passive vocabulary words are rather easily available to us, while others are available only with great time and effort, and still others are entirely beyond our reach. Psychologists call these dredging-up stages "degrees of availability," and we know intuitively that each of us has an availability threshold for terms in our passive vocabulary, a threshold that can only be crossed after goal-directed rehearsal and practice. Some of us, for instance, who are not crossword puzzle addicts may have a large passive vocabulary and yet stumble over a puzzle for hours, whereas a crossword habitué who is less literate than ourselves may polish off the puzzle in twenty minutes. Years of rehearsal have greatly enlarged the individual's easily available vocabulary without greatly changing his or her total lexicon.

Now, to get back to my thought-experiment, let us suppose that research has determined how much rehearsal time it takes on the average to make a discernible improvement in the degree of availability for each of the subskills of writing. I am not claiming of course that these subskills are precisely defined and settled right now; I'm just *pretending* that they are in order to create a plausible model like that shown in Table 1.

You will immediately notice that a discernible development of all these subskills will take longer than a college semester. Notice also that the weeks listed on the chart are quantum times—that is, they are the minimum times needed to effect any lasting improvement at all in the *availability* of the subskill named. So if you don't take at least that much time, even under optimum conditions, you might as well neglect the subskill entirely. Under these circumstances, the crucial question we then must face is this: Which of these skills should we teach in a one-shot semester course and which ones should we neglect? We cannot teach them all. My guess is that if we had only the information listed on this chart, we would have some rather vigorous and familiar controversies on our hands when we tried to answer that question.

But I will carry the thought-experiment further and pretend that we also have some additional research results of impeccable reliability. These fictitious results are summarized in Table 2.

Now I'll ask you to ignore the particular subskills named on the left-hand side (since they were chosen somewhat arbitrarily) and concentrate your attention on the items on the right-hand side of the chart. They represent the results of tests given to two comparable basic writing student populations after they had been instructed for a semester in these two different curricula. The tests were conducted as follows. On the first day of testing, the students were given a choice of topics and told they had to write a three-page draft in forty-five minutes, without making any corrections on the first draft. On the second day they were allowed one hour to rewrite the original draft. On the third day they were allowed up to three hours to revise and rewrite their

Table 1

Quantum Time for Improvement in Writing Skills
of Basic Writing Students*

Subskill of Writing	Average Quantum Time to Reach Improvement in Availability of Skill
Usage	4 weeks
Sentence variety	3 weeks
Invention techniques	2 weeks
Arrangement principles	2 weeks
Paragraphing	3 weeks
Genre-audience conventions	5 weeks
Coherence devices	2 weeks
Focusing devices	2 weeks
Analytical reading skills	5 weeks
Total	28 weeks

*Assumptions: age group 17-21 and optimum teaching methods for each skill. Grapholectic skills, such as spelling and punctuation, and dialect-interference problems addressed in self-paced outside sessions.

papers. Thus, the numbers on the right-hand side represent the average test scores for each day for students who had undergone the two patterns of instruction. Group One, as you see, could do a lot better than Group Two in a rapid first draft. Then in the revised draft on the second test, the groups were about equal, but Group Two did significantly better when students took as much time as they wanted for a final revision.

A Hypothetical Consensus

In a moment I will suggest why this kind of experimental result is not purely whimsical and implausible. But first I will state the main inference to be drawn from the thought-experiment. It is the point which I have made a theme of my remarks, namely the idea that we will argue less when good research teaches us more. If all of us really trusted the above results—if, for instance, they had been tested and duplicated even by researchers who were initially hostile or unpersuaded—I think that we would *not* divide into camps over these two curricular patterns. We would very quickly form a consensus that Curriculum II is superior to Curriculum I, for, we would agree, first of all, that an 85 is better than a 60. We would also understand that these final numbers identify the level of skill attained, though not of course the level of facility. We would understand that students' *facility* in writing would automatically increase in both cases if they continued their writing outside the classroom, whereas their *level* of skill might not increase merely by further writing. Just in case some skeptics still refused to

Table 2

Two Instructional Patterns Compared*

Curricula	Test Results
I: Invention (2 weeks); Arrangement (2 weeks); Sentence variety (3 weeks); Genre-audience conventions (5 weeks); coherence devices (2 weeks). Total: 14 weeks.	1st version: 50 2nd version: 55 3rd version: 60
II: Invention (2 weeks); Arrangement (2 weeks); Paragraphing (3 weeks); Analytical reading (5 weeks); Focusing devices (2 weeks). Total: 14 weeks.	1st version: 20 2nd version: 55 3rd version: 85

*Assumptions: age group 17-21 and optimum teaching methods for each skill. Grapholectic skills, such as spelling and punctuation, and dialect-interference problems addressed in self-paced outside sessions.

be persuaded at this point, we would conduct further research to determine what happened to history and English majors two years later, after they had been writing a number of papers in college courses. The results of this hypothetical research are shown in Table 3.

By the time this study had been well-publicized, we can be confident that a consensus would have been established favoring Curriculum II over Curriculum I, always assuming that we had confidence in the reliability of the research behind the studies. Thenceforward, our controversies over that particular question will have simply disappeared. Where before zealous partisans expended their energies in polemics, their energies would now be directed towards still more refined curricula that are superior even to Curriculum II. In other words, we would have become, as Kuhn would say, a mature discipline in which passion and zeal no longer substituted for lack of information.

Cost-Benefit Analysis of Writing Skills

Before I leave my utopian thought-model, I want to make just a few, very brief remarks about the structure of my imaginary experiment. Many readers will have been rightly skeptical of its structure because they will have doubted that the complex skill of writing can be so neatly broken down into teachable subskills. They might suspect that growth in writing is an organic process rather than an atomistic one such as my model suggests. This is a highly plausible view, and it is fruitless to argue its pros and cons in our present state of ignorance. But I do want

Table 3

Two Instructional Patterns Compared
after Two Years*

Curricula	Test Results
Curriculum I	1st version: 57 2nd version: 65 3rd version: 70
Curriculum II	1st version: 57 2nd version: 75 3rd version: 90

*Assumption: post-test limited to history and English majors after two full years of college course work.

to suggest one aspect of my model which psychologists have established pretty firmly. Learners have a very limited channel capacity at any moment of time. Their circuits can get very easily overloaded if they are asked to perform several unfamiliar routines at the same time. When the mind does get overloaded in this way, an interesting phenomenon occurs: one's performance in every subroutine, even in a familiar one, is degraded. For instance, if you are a good speller, but are asked to write a first draft on a difficult topic, your spelling will decline along with your style, whereas both your spelling and style will be superior in a first draft on a familiar and easy topic.

This principle of overloading explains why it is plausible to find the kind of differences that I posited in the test results, when students are permitted unlimited time to revise their papers. Each time they revise and edit they can pay attention to a different aspect of writing without overloading their circuits. Given unlimited time, students who can best *read and criticize* their own writings will probably *compose* the best papers, even though they might perform very badly in the first draft. In other words, the various subskills of writing may plausibly be submitted to a cost-benefit analysis, showing that the teaching of some skills may lead faster to higher levels of writing ability than the teaching of other skills.

There is an analogy for such cost-benefit evaluation in the history of writing as a purely physical motor skill. Suppose we wanted to make a cost-benefit analysis of teaching the Chinese ideographic script as compared with the Roman alphabetic script. And let us suppose that two writers of equal dexterity, one Chinese, the other American, were asked to copy out in their own language the first chapter of the Book of Genesis. Using modern ideographs, the Chinese writer would quickly leave the American in the dust. For every stroke made by the Chinese writer, the American would need to make four strokes. Without a doubt, modern Chinese ideographs are more conducive to purely scribal *fluency* than modern alphabetic scripts.

But when we look at the two methods from the learner's standpoint, we get a different result. The 26 characters of the alphabetic script might be learned in two weeks, whereas the 44,000 ideographs of Chinese, for all its final fluency, would require two or three years at least. Now by analogy, if we have just thirteen weeks in college composition courses, we are well advised to prefer the teaching of a few basic and constantly usable principles over the teaching of many local and limited fluencies. In composition skills, of course, no such clear-cut comparison is possible. But we do need to accept the truth that limited time forces us to make trade-offs and to make choices which we do not yet know how to make. To gain this kind of knowledge is a research goal of high priority and will certainly bring us closer to a consensus over teaching aims and methods.

The Importance of Evaluation

It is obvious, however, that no such knowledge could ever be gained if we could not evaluate the quality of writing educed by the different methods of instruction. And so I will go out on a limb on the subject of evaluation, a subject that is currently the focus of my own research. It is also a subject with ramifications that go far beyond research and start far earlier than college composition courses. For many reasons I think evaluation is our most pressing problem, both in teaching and research.

In the classroom, from grade school to college, the judge of writing quality is the teacher—the grade giver. This powerful personage works in such mysterious and unpredictable ways that to move from one teacher's writing class to another's can be like traveling from Poland to Peru. One teacher grades you down if you use the first-person singular, another grades you down if you don't. One marks you way up for correctness, another for ideas, still another for an expressive style or, contrariwise, for a neutral style. Students hold the universal belief that an A paper in one writing section will be a C paper in another and vice versa. The reason that their belief is universal is that it is empirically true.

That student folklore is correct on this point was demonstrated some years ago by Diederich in an experiment with 300 student papers. I will remind you of just one of his results. On a nine-point rank ordering (that is, putting the papers in nine piles in order of merit), 34 percent of the papers received every ranking from one to nine; 94 percent of them received either seven, eight, or nine different rankings. No essay received less than five different rankings.

Undoubtedly, these results could be greatly improved on in a particular institution in a particular multisectioned course through grading sessions among the teachers. We hold such sessions at my own university, and we always get more consistent results afterwards than we got before. But that is only because, in the end, our group has agreed to adopt the principles of our course director, not because we are persuaded that those principles correspond to our own.

The main reason, then, for the baffling mystery of the composition class to the student is the bewildering variation among composition teachers in doctrine and grading. It is but a small step for a student to move from bafflement to anxiety, and most of us still harbor some of those childhood anxieties over the mysteries and imperatives of writing. We can easily understand why students take those further downward steps from anxiety to defeatism to the total waning of motivation.

Pedagogical Polemics and Research

So much for the way our "methods" of evaluation can affect the teaching and learning of composition. Our methods also deeply affect the quality of the research designed to improve the teaching of composition. Anyone well read in the literature of composition research will be familiar with the success rate of new pedagogical methods as tested out by their proponents. As far as my reading extends, the success rate is 100 percent. The trouble is, we cannot trust these results. We cannot be sure of their duplicability or their inherent validity, because we cannot trust the principles of evaluation on which the judgments of "experienced readers" were based. The readers themselves would be hard pressed to enumerate their principles when challenged to do so. I say this with some confidence, because I once asked the Chief Reader at the Educational Testing Service to explain his grading principles, and he was able to explain only his method for getting his Table Leaders to agree with him. In short, we cannot as yet rely on any research that evaluates the *relative* merits of teaching methods in composition. On the other hand, if the problem of intrinsic evaluation can be solved (and it is at least solvable in principle), then we will be able to have intercomparable results in research. Our empirical knowledge will be put on a sounder footing. Should that happy day arrive, how pointless will seem our lack of consensus over questions that are essentially testable and empirical.

What, for instance, does our banner cry *"process, not product"* really amount to? Part of its success as a slogan must come from its alliteration rather than its content, since not one of us would stick up for any method of instruction that we firmly knew to be an inferior method in the teaching of writing. Nor would any of us who now stress the idea of process wish to do so if we thought that it bore no relation to product.

Some time ago, in my first years as a director of freshman English, I had my own polemical axe to grind under the slogan "composition, not literature, in the composition class." I knew at the time that those who stressed literature did so less from wickedness than from desperation at not knowing *how* to teach writing. On the other side, so zealous was I in my campaign against putting literature in the composition course that I overlooked the obvious truth that teaching literature can mean, when responsibly done, the teaching of *reading*. And it is inherently obvious that we cannot write better than we can read. Some educators propose writing instruction as a good technique for reading instruction, and there is every reason to think that the opposite method is also valid—valid enough, certainly, to cool down my earlier zeal and partisanship against teaching analytical reading in the writing class. That's another issue we need to learn more about and another illustration of the intimate connection between partisan zeal and lack of knowledge.

The cure for ignorance is of course good research and the promulgation of its fruits. From research already conducted, we can guess that many of our controversies will end in intelligent compromise, as, for instance, the controversies of process versus product and literature versus composition. While we cannot expect significant research advances on a broad front until we agree on standard measuring principles, we can nonetheless state some of the criteria that good composition research ought to meet if it is to yield us the knowledge that we so desperately need.

Definitiveness and Generativeness

The minimal criterion of good composition research would be *definitiveness*. A definitive piece of work is simply one that will never have to be done over again. It is research that provides an answer to a question that has been so carefully framed that no significant loose ends (extraneous variables) are left over which might permit a different result. If other researchers in another time and place were to repeat the work, they would also repeat the results. In short, definitiveness means reliability, an elementary criterion for all good empirical work.

If, for example, a researcher finds that a teaching technique combining workshops with tutorials is better than one combining classes and conferences, then it ought to be shown that anyone who repeated the experiment with that age group would get the same results. But for this to be shown, the experimental method and the evaluative technique must have been so carefully described and controlled that any distant researcher would duplicate the results independently.

Suppose for a moment that this work on tutorials had been accomplished definitively for the first time. It would then automatically meet an even loftier criterion for good research—that of *generativeness*, by which I mean research that not only leads to practical applications, but also opens up whole domains of further research. If, for instance, our researcher on tutorials had devised a way of cancelling out extraneous variables, this newly developed technique would have many applications for future experimental designs. The researcher would have solved a problem, in this case a methodological one, which opened up research possibilities which had not existed before.

Most good research in well-developed empirical fields must be content to satisfy the criterion of definitiveness. Only very lucky or very gifted researchers can make generative contributions. Yet our field is so virginal and so rich in significant possibilities that many in the 1980s may have a chance to make generative discoveries. And even if not, the ideal of significant definitive research is itself an inspiring one, especially when our research opportunities are compared to those that exist in the trodden paths of literary interpretation. Most of us, when we entered graduate school, did not forsee ourselves as engaging in the kind of research required by the problems that we now recognize as most important, namely the problems of literacy rather than those of literature. But if our profession takes us into realms that we could not have predicted when we started out, that makes our enterprise all the more adventurous and compelling.

12 Selected Bibliography: Composition and Basic Writing

Daniel R. Hoeber
Mercy College of Detroit

Arden, J. W., and W. A. Terrell. *Research and Development of English Programs in the Junior College.* Urbana, Ill.: NCTE, 1965.

Baron, Dennis E. "Non-Standard English, Composition, and the Academic Establishment." *College English* 37 (1975): 176-183.

Bateman, Donald, and Frank Zidonis. *The Effect of a Study of Transformational Grammar on the Writing of Ninth and Tenth Graders.* Research Report No. 6. Urbana, Ill.: NCTE, 1966.

Bentley, Robert H., and Samuel D. Crawford, eds. *Black Language Reader.* Glenview, Ill.: Scott, Foresman, 1973.

Bernadette, Sr. Miriam. "Evaluation of Writing: A Three-Part Program." *English Journal* 54 (1965): 23-27.

Block, J. H., ed. *Mastery Learning: Theory and Practice.* New York: Holt, 1971.

Bloom, Benjamin S., et al. *Handbook of Formative and Summative Evaluation of Student Learning.* New York: McGraw-Hill, 1971.

Bloom, Sophie. *Peer and Cross-Age Tutoring in the Schools.* Washington, D. C.: National Institute of Education, DHEW, 1976.

Blumenthal, Joseph C. *English 2600.* 3rd ed. New York: Harcourt, Brace, 1960.

Blumenthal, Joseph C. *English 3200.* 2nd ed. New York: Harcourt Brace Jovanovich, 1972.

Bormuth, John R. *On the Theory of Achievement Test Items.* Chicago: University of Chicago Press, 1970.

Bossone, Richard M., and Lynn Q. Troyka. *A Strategy for Coping with High School and Remedial English Problems.* New York: Center for Advanced Studies in Eduation, 1976.

Bossone, Richard M., and Max Weiner. *City University English Teachers: A Self-Report Regarding Remedial Teaching.* New York: CUNY Graduate School and University Center, 1975.

Braddock, Richard, Richard Lloyd-Jones, and Lowell Schoer. *Research in Written Composition.* Urbana, Ill.: NCTE, 1963.

Brause, Rita S. "Developmental Aspects of the Ability to Understand Semantic Ambiguity, with Implications for Teachers." *Research in the Teaching of English* 11 (1977): 39-48.

Brown, Rexford. "Measuring Growth and Proficiency in Writing." *Journal of Basic Writing,* CCNY (Fall, 1978).

Selected Bibliography

Brown, Rexford. *Writing Mechanics, 1969-1974*. Denver: National Assessment of Educational Progress, 1976.

Bruffee, Kenneth. "A New Intellectual Frontier: Point of View." *The Chronicle of Higher Education*, 27 February 1978, p. 40.

Bruffee, Kenneth. *A Short Course in Writing*. Cambridge, Mass.: Winthrop, 1972.

Buros, O. K., ed. *The Seventh Mental Measurements Yearbook*. Edison, N. J.: Gryphon Press, 1972.

Butler, Eugenia. *An Auto-Instructional Text in Correct Writing*. 2nd ed. Lexington, Mass.: D. C. Heath, 1975.

Butler, Melvin A., chair. *Students' Right to Their Own Language*. Urbana, Ill.: NCTE, 1974.

California Association of Teachers of English. *A Scale of Evaluation of High School Student Essays*. Champaign, Ill.: NCTE, 1960.

Campbell, Dianna S., and Terry Ryan Meier. "A Design for a Developmental Writing Course for Academically Underprepared Black Students." *Journal of Basic Writing* 2 (1976): 20-30.

Carkhuff, Robert R. *Helping and Human Relations: A Primer for Lay and Professional Helpers*. 2 vols. New York: Holt, 1969.

Cast, B. D. M. "The Efficiency of Different Methods of Marking English Compositions." *British Journal of Educational Psychology* 9 (1939): 257-269; 10 (1940): 49-60.

Chaikas, Elaine. "Who Can Be Taught?" *College English* 35 (1974): 574-583.

Chomsky, Carol. "Stages in Language Development and Reading Exposure." *Harvard Educational Review* 42 (1972): 1-33.

Christensen, Francis, with Bonniejean Christensen. *Notes toward a New Rhetoric: Nine Essays for Teachers*. 2nd ed. New York: Harper and Row, 1978.

Clapp, Ouida, ed. *Classroom Practices in Teaching English, 1977-78: Teaching the Basics—Really!* Urbana, Ill.: NCTE, 1977.

Cohen, Arthur M. "Assessing College Students' Ability to Write Compositions." *Research in the Teaching of English* 7 (1973): 356-371.

Coleman, James, et al. *Equality of Educational Opportunity*. Washington, D. C.: U. S. Government Printing Office, 1966.

Coleman, James, et al. *Youth: Transition to Adulthood*. Chicago: University of Chicago Press, 1974.

Coles, William E., Jr. *The Plural I*. New York: Holt, 1978.

Cooper, Charles R. "Measuring Growth in Writing." *English Journal* 64 (1975): 111-119.

Cooper, Charles R. "An Outline for Writing Sentence-Combining Problems." *English Journal* 62 (1973): 96-102, 108.

Cooper, Charles R., and Lee Odell, eds. *Evaluating Writing: Describing, Measuring, Judging*. Urbana, Ill.: NCTE, 1977.

Cooper, Charles R., and Lee Odell, eds. *Research on Composing: Points of Departure*. Urbana, Ill.: NCTE, 1978.

Cowan, Gregory. *An Annotated List of Training Programs for Community College English Teachers: A CCCC Report*. Urbana, Ill.: ERIC/RCS, ERIC/JC, and CCCC, 1977.

Coward, Ann F. "A Comparison of Two Methods of Grading English Compositions." *Journal of Educational Research* 46 (1952): 81-93.

Cross, K. Patricia. *Accent on Learning*. San Francisco: Jossey-Bass, 1976.

Cross, K. Patricia. *Beyond the Open Door*. San Francisco: Jossey-Bass, 1971.

Cross, K. Patricia. *The Junior College Student: A Research Description*. Princeton, N. J.: Educational Testing Service, 1968.

Daiker, D., et al. "Sentence Combining and Syntactic Maturity in Freshman English." *College Composition and Communication* 29 (1978): 36-41.

Dauterman, Fritz P. "Syntactic Maturity Test for Narrative Writing." ERIC ED 091 757.

Davidson, David M. "Sentence Combining in an ESL Writing Program." *Journal of Basic Writing* 3 (1975): 49-62.

Davies, Alan, ed. *Problems of Language and Learning*. London: Heineman, 1975.

Davis, Junius A., et al. *The Impact of Special Services Programs in Higher Education for Disadvantaged Students*. Princeton, N. J.: Educational Testing Service, 1975.

D'Eloia, Sarah. "Teaching Standard Written English." *Journal of Basic Writing* 1 (1975): 5-13.

Desy, Jeanne. "Reasoned Writing for Basic Students: A Course Design." *Journal of Basic Writing* 2 (1976): 4-19.

Diederich, Paul B. "Cooperative Preparation and Rating of Essay Tests." ERIC ED 091 750.

Diederich, Paul B. "Grading and Measuring." ERIC ED 031 479.

Diederich, Paul B. *Measuring Growth in English*. Urbana, Ill.: NCTE, 1974.

Diederich, Paul B., et al. *Factors in Judgment of Writing Ability*. Princeton, N. J.: Educational Testing Service, 1961.

Dixon, Edward. "Indexes of Syntactic Maturity." ERIC ED 091 748.

Dugger, Ronnie. "Cooperative Learning in a Writing Community." *Change*, July 1976, pp. 30-33.

Eagle, Norman. "Validity of Student Ratings: A Reaction." *Community and Junior College Journal* 46 (1975): 6-8.

Elgin, Suzette Haden. "Don't No Revolutions Hardly *Ever* Come by Here." *College English* 39 (1978): 784-790.

Elley, W. B., et al. "The Role of Grammar in a Secondary School English Curriculum." *Research in the Teaching of English* 10 (1976): 5-21.

Emig, Janet. *The Composing Processes of Twelfth Graders*. Research Report No. 13. Urbana, Ill.: NCTE, 1971.

English Modular Mini-Courses. Santa Monica, Calif.: Educational Tutorial Systems, 1973.

Fagan, William T., Charles R. Cooper, and Julie M. Jensen, eds. *Measures for Research and Evaluation in the English Language Arts*. Urbana, Ill.: ERIC/RCS and NCTE, 1975.

Farrell, Thomas J. "Open Admissions, Orality, and Literacy." *Journal of Youth and Adolescence* 3 (1974): 247-260.

Farrell, Thomas J. "Reading in the Community College." *College English* 37 (1975): 40-46.

Selected Bibliography

Fasold, Ralph W., and Roger W. Shuy, eds. *Teaching Standard English in the Inner City.* Washington, D. C.: Center for Applied Linguistics, 1970.

Fawcett, Susan C., and Alvin Sandberg. *Grassroots: The Writer's Workbook.* Boston: Houghton Mifflin, 1976.

Fergus, Patricia M. *Spelling Improvement: A Program for Self-Instruction.* New York: McGraw-Hill, 1973.

Finn, J. D. "Expectations and the Educational Environment." *Journal of Educational Research* 48 (1972): 387-410.

Fogg, C. P. "Boston University's College of Basic Studies: A Non-Traditional Approach Which Successfully Serves Marginal Applicants." *Perspectives* 7 (1973): 45-99.

Folger, John, et al. *Human Resources and Higher Education.* New York: Russell Sage Foundation, 1970.

Frank, Marcella. *Modern English: Exercises for Non-Native Speakers. Part 1: Parts of Speech.* Englewood Cliffs, N. J.: Prentice-Hall, 1972.

Frank, Marcella. *Modern English: Exercises for Non-Native Speakers. Part 2: Sentences and Complex Structures.* Englewood Cliffs, N. J.: Prentice-Hall, 1972.

Gage, N. L., ed. *Handbook of Research on Teaching.* Chicago: Rand McNally, 1963.

Gefvert, Constance, Richard Raspa, and Amy Richards. *Keys to American English.* New York: Harcourt Brace Jovanovich, 1975.

Glazier, Teresa Ferster. *The Least You Should Know About English.* New York: Holt, 1977.

Godshalk, Fred I., Frances Swineford, and William E. Coffman. *The Measurement of Writing Ability.* New York: College Entrance Examination Board, 1966.

Gordon, Edmund W. *Opportunity Programs for the Disadvantaged in Higher Education.* Washington, D. C.: American Association for Higher Education, 1975.

Gordon, Edmund W., and Doxey Wilkerson. *Compensatory Education for the Disadvantaged.* New York: College Entrance Examination Board, 1966.

Gorrell, Robert M. "Not by Nature: Approaches to Rhetoric." *English Journal* 55 (1969): 409-416, 449.

Gorrell, Robert M., and Charlton Laird. *The Modern English Handbook.* 6th ed. Englewood Cliffs, N. J.: Prentice-Hall, 1976.

Gowan, James A. *English Review Manual.* New York: McGraw-Hill, 1970.

Grant, Mary Kathryn, and Daniel R. Hoeber. *Basic Skills Programs: Are They Working?* Washington, D. C.: American Association for Higher Education, 1978.

Green, Thomas L. *The Activities of Teaching.* New York: McGraw-Hill, 1971.

Griffin, Jacqueline. "Remedial Composition at an Open Door College." *College Composition and Communication* 20 (1967): 360-363.

Gronlund, Norman E. *Constructing Achievement Tests.* Englewood Cliffs, N. J.: Prentice-Hall, 1968.

Gronlund, Norman E. *Measurement and Evaluation in Testing.* New York: Macmillan, 1971.

Halsted, Isabella. "Putting Error in Its Place." *Journal of Basic Writing* 1 (1975): 72-86.

Hartwell, Patrick. "The Great Punctuation Game." *Freshman English News* 6 (1979), forthcoming.

Hartwell, Patrick, and Robet Bentley. *Open to Language: A College Rhetoric.* New York: Oxford University Press, forthcoming.

Herrscher, Barton R. *Implementing Individualized Instruction.* Houston, Tex.: ArChem Publishers, 1971.

Higgins, John A. "Remedial Students' Needs vs. Emphasis in Text-Workbooks." *College Composition and Communication* 24 (1973): 188-192.

Hirasawa, Louise, and Linda Markstein. *Developing Reading Skills: Advanced.* Rowley, Mass.: Newberry House, 1974.

Hirsch, E. D., Jr. *The Philosophy of Composition.* Chicago: University of Chicago Press, 1977.

Horn, Thomas, ed. *Research Bases for Oral Language Instruction.* Urbana, Ill.: NCTE, 1971.

Howland, Larry, and Steve Bannow, eds. *The Writing Laboratory Report and Handbook.* 2 vols. Columbia: University of South Carolina, 1977.

Hunt, Kellogg W. *Grammatical Structures Written at Three Grade Levels.* Research Report No. 3. Urbana, Ill.: NCTE, 1965.

Hunt, Kellogg W. "A Synopsis of Clause-to-Sentence Length Factors." *English Journal* 54 (1965): 300, 305-309.

Hunt, Kellogg W. "Syntactic Maturity in School Children and Adults." *Monographs of the Society of Research in Child Development,* Vol. 31, No. 134 (1970).

Irmscher, William F. "The Teaching of Writing in Terms of Growth." *English Journal* 66 (1977): 33-36.

Jaffe, A. J., and Walter Adams. *Academic Socio-Economic Factors Related to Entrance and Retention at Two- and Four-Year Colleges in the Late 60's.* Washington, D. C.: Bureau of Applied Social Resources, Office of Education, DHEW, 1970.

Johnson, G. R. "Teacher Preparation for Community/Junior Colleges." *Community/Junior College Research Quarterly* 1 (1977): 249-256.

Johnson, Nancy W. "The Uses of Grammatical and Rhetorical Norms, Pedagogical Strategies and Statistical Methods in Designing and Validating a Composition Placement Instrument." Doctor of Arts dissertation, Catholic University of America, 1976.

Johnson, Paula, and Judith D. Hackman. "The Yale Average, or, After Competence, What?" *College Composition and Communication* 29 (1978): 47-52.

Judine, Sr. M., ed. *A Guide for Evaluating Student Composition.* Urbana, Ill.: NCTE, 1965.

Kasden, Lawrence. "Chairing a Two-Year College English Department." *ADE/MLA Bulletin,* September 1978, pp. 14-19.

Katz, I. "Academic Motivation and Equal Educational Opportunity." *Harvard Educational Review* 33 (1968): 57-65.

Kehoe, Josephine. "Compassionate Grading: Possible?" *Arizona English Bulletin* 16 (1974): 146-151.

King, Martha L. "Research in Composition: A Need for Theory." *Research in the Teaching of English* 12 (1978): 193-202.

Koch, Carl, and James M. Brazil. *Strategies for Teaching the Composition Process.* Urbana, Ill.: NCTE, 1978.

Kochman, Thomas. "Cross-Cultural Communication: Contrasting Perspectives, Conflicting Sensibilities." *Florida FL Reporter* 9 (1971): 3-16, 53-54.

Krishna, Valerie. "The Syntax of Error." *Journal of Basic Writing* 1 (1975): 43-49.

Kuhn, Thomas S. *The Structure of Scientific Revolutions.* 2nd ed. Foundations of the Unity of Science Series. Vol. 2, No. 2. Chicago: University of Chicago Press, 1970.

Labov, William. *Language in the Inner City: Studies in the Black English Vernacular.* Philadelphia: University of Pennsylvania Press, 1972.

Labov, William. *The Study of Nonstandard English.* Urbana, Ill.: NCTE, Center for Applied Linguistics, and ERIC, 1970.

Larson, Richard L. "Selected Bibliography of Research and Writing about the Teaching of Composition, 1978." *College Composition and Communication* 30 (1979): 196-213.

Lattin, Vernon E. "A Program for Basic Writing." *College English* 40 (1978): 312-317.

Laurence, Patricia. "Error's Endless Train: Why Students Don't Perceive Errors." *Journal of Basic Writing* 1 (1975): 23-42.

Lauria, A. R. *Cognitive Development: Its Cultural and Social Foundations.* Cambridge, Mass.: Harvard University Press, 1976.

Lay, Nancy. "Chinese Language Interference in Written English." *Journal of Basic Writing* 1 (1975): 50-61.

Lenning, Oscar T., ed. *New Directions for Higher Education: Improving Student Outcomes.* San Francisco: Jossey-Bass, 1976.

Lester, Mark. "The Value of Transformational Grammar in Teaching Composition." *College Composition and Communication* 18 (1967): 227-231.

McColly, William. "Composition Rating Scales for General Merit." *Journal of Educational Research* 59 (1965): 55-66.

McColly, William. "What Does Educational Research Say about the Judgment of Writing Ability?" *Journal of Educational Research* 64 (1970): 148-154.

McDonald, W. V. "Grading Student Writing." *College Composition and Communication* 25 (1975): 154-158.

McFarland, Betty. "An Alternative Program for Basic Composition Courses." Paper read at Southeastern Conference on English in the Two-Year College, 17 February 1978, Nashville, Tenn.

McFarland, Betty. "Counterstatement." *Teaching English in the Two-Year College* 2 (1976): 179-180.

McFarland, Betty. "An Individualized Course in Elementary Composition for the Marginal Student." In *Personalized Instruction in Higher Education: Proceedings of the Second National Conference*, pp. 45-48. Ed. Ben A. Green, Jr., 1976.

McFarland, Betty. "The Non-Credit Writing Laboratory." *Teaching English in the Two-Year College* 1 (1975): 153-154.

McFarland, Betty. *Writing and Proofreading: Priority #4.* Boone, N. C.: Appalachian State University English Department, 1973.

McQuade, Donald, ed. *Language and Style.* Akron, Ohio: University of Akron Press, forthcoming.

Macrorie, Ken. *Telling Writing.* 2nd ed. New York: Hayden, 1976.

Medsker, Leland L. *The Junior College: Progress and Prospect.* New York: McGraw-Hill, 1960.

Mellon, John C. *Transformational Sentence Combining: A Method for Enhancing the Development of Syntactic Fluency in English Composition.* Urbana, Ill.: NCTE, 1969.

Mills, Helen. *Commanding Paragraphs.* Glenview, Ill.: Scott, Foresman, 1976.

Mills, Helen. *Commanding Sentences: A Charted Course in Basic Writing Skills.* Glenview, Ill.: Scott, Foresman, 1974.

Mills, Helen. "Language and Composition: Three Mastery Learning Courses in One Classroom." *Journal of Basic Writing* 2 (1976): 44-59.

Mink, Oscar G. *The Behavior Change Process.* New York: Harper and Row, 1970.

Moment, Maureen. "A Description of the Writing of English 1000 Students at Virginia Polytechnic Institute and State University." M.A. thesis, Virginia Polytechnic Institute, 1978.

Moore, William, Jr. *Community College Response to the High Risk Student: A Critical Reappraisal.* Washington, D. C.: American Association of Community-Junior Colleges, 1976.

Mosteller, F., and Daniel P. Moynihan, eds. *On Equality of Educational Opportunity.* New York: Random House, 1972.

Mulka, Mary Janet, and Edmund J. Sheerin. *An Evaluation of Policy-Related Research on Postsecondary Education for the Disadvantaged.* 2 vols. Washington, D. C.: National Science Foundation, 1974.

Mullis, I. *The Primary Trait System for Scoring Writing Tasks.* Denver: National Assessment of Educational Progress, 1976.

Neel, Jasper P., and Jeanne C. Nelson. "From the Editor." *ADE Bulletin* 56 (1978): i-iii.

Newman, F., et al. *Report on Higher Education.* Washington, D. C.: U.S. Government Printing Office, 1971.

Nisbet, J. D. "English Composition in Secondary School Selection." *British Journal of Educational Psychology* 25 (1955): 51-54.

Noreen, R. G. "Placement Procedures for Freshman Composition."*College Composition and Communication* 28 (1977): 141-144.

O'Hare, Frank. *Sentence Combining: Improving Student Writing without Formal Grammar Instruction.* Research Report No. 15. Urbana, Ill.: NCTE, 1973.

Ohmann, Richard. *English in America: A Radical View of the Profession.* New York: Oxford University Press, 1976.

Ong, Walter J., S. J. "Literacy and Orality in Our Times." *ADE Bulletin* 58 (1978): 1-7.

Palmer, W. S. "Measuring Written Expression: Quality Scales and the Sentence." *High School Journal* 60 (1976): 32-40.

Selected Bibliography

Perrin, Porter G. *Handbook of Current English.* 3rd ed. Glenview, Ill.: Scott, Foresman, 1968.

Perrine, Laurence, ed. *Story and Structure.* 4th ed. New York: Harcourt Brace Jovanovich, 1974.

Petrie, Anne. "Teaching the Thinking Process in Essay Writing." *Journal of Basic Writing* 2 (1976): 60-67.

Petrosky, Anthony R. "Grammar Instruction—What We Know." *English Journal* 66 (1977): 86-89.

Pierog, Paul. "Coaching Writing." *Journal of Basic Writing* 2 (1976): 68-77.

Ponsot, Marie. "Total Immersion." *Journal of Basic Writing* 2 (1976): 31-43.

Potter, Robert R. *Language Workshop.* New York: Globe, 1976.

Pritchard, N. S. "The Training of the Junior College English Teacher." *College Composition and Communication* 21 (1970): 48-54.

Purves, Alan, and the Task Force on Measurement and Evaluation in the Study of English. *Common Sense and Testing in English.* Urbana, Ill.: NCTE, 1975.

Ravan, Frances Ondee. "An Analytic Study of the Essay Test of the Language Skills Examination in the Georgia Rising Junior Testing Program." Ed.D. dissertation, University of Georgia, 1973.

Rizzo, Betty, and Santiago Villafane. "Spanish Influence on Written English." *Journal of Basic Writing* 1 (1975): 62-71.

Rosenthal, Robert. "Self-Fulfilling Prophecy." *Psychology Today* 2 (1968): 44-51.

Rosenthal, Robert, and Lenore Jacobson. *Pygmalion in the Classroom: Teacher Expectation and the Pupil's Intellectual Development.* New York: Holt, 1968.

Ross, Janet, and Gladys Doty. *Writing English: A Composition Text in English as a Foreign Language.* 2nd ed. New York: Harper and Row, 1975.

Roueche, John E. "Accommodating Individual Differences." *Community College Review* 1 (1973): 24-29.

Roueche, John E. "Creating an Environment for Learning." *Community and Junior College Journal* 46 (1976): 48-50.

Roueche, John E. "Feeling Good about Yourself: What Is Effective Remedial Education?" *Community College Frontiers* 4 (1976): 10-13.

Roueche, John E., ed. *New Directions for Higher Education: Increasing Basic Skills by Developmental Studies.* San Francisco: Jossey-Bass, 1977.

Roueche, John E., and Barton Herrscher, eds. *Toward Instructional Accountability.* Palo Alto, Calif.: Westinghouse Learning Corp., 1973.

Roueche, John E., Barton Herrscher, and George A. Baker. *Time as the Variable, Achievement as the Constant: Competency Based Instruction in the Community College.* Washington, D. C.: American Association of Community-Junior Colleges, 1976.

Roueche, John E., and R. Wade Kirk. *Catching Up: Remedial Education.* San Francisco: Jossey-Bass, 1973.

Roueche, John E., and Oscar G. Mink. *Improving Student Motivation.* Austin, Tex.: Sterling Swift, 1976.

Roueche, John E., and Oscar G. Mink. "Toward Personhood Development in the Community College." *Community College Review* 3 (1976): 40-50.

Roueche, John E., and Suanne D. Roueche. *Developmental Education: A Primer for Program Development and Education.* Atlanta: Southern Regional Education Board, 1977.

Roueche, John E., and Jerry J. Snow. *Overcoming Learning Problems: A Guide to Developmental Education in College.* San Francisco: Jossey-Bass, 1977.

Sanford, Nevitt, ed. *The American College.* New York: Wiley, 1962.

Schwartz, William, and Serapio R. Zalba, eds. *The Practice of Group Work.* New York: Columbia University Press, 1971.

Shaughnessy, Mina. "Diving In: An Introduction to Basic Writing." *College Composition and Communication* 27 (1976): 234-239.

Shaughnessy, Mina. *Errors and Expectations: A Guide for the Teacher of Basic Writing.* New York: Oxford University Press, 1977.

Shaughnessy, Mina. "Some Needed Research on Writing." *College Composition and Communication* 28 (1977): 317-320.

Sherwin, J. Stephen. *Four Problems in Teaching English: A Critique of Research.* Scranton, Pa.: International Textbook, 1969.

Shuy, Roger. *Field Techniques in an Urban Language Study.* Washington, D. C.: Center for Applied Linguistics, 1968.

Shuy, Roger. *Social Dialect and Language Learning.* Urbana, Ill.: NCTE, 1964.

Sims, Odette P. *Spelling: Patterns of Sound.* New York: McGraw-Hill, 1974.

Singer, Harry, and Robert B. Ruddel, eds. *Theoretical Models and Processes of Reading.* 2nd ed. Newark, Del.: International Reading Association, 1976.

Sledd, James. "Bidialectalism: The Linguistics of White Supremacy." *English Journal* 58 (1969): 1311-1317.

Slotnick, Henry B. "An Examination of the Computer Grading of Essays." Ph.D. dissertation, University of Illinois at Urbana-Champaign, 1971.

Smith, Eugene H. *Teacher Preparation in Composition.* Urbana, Ill.: NCTE, 1969.

Smith, Frank. *Understanding Reading.* 2nd ed. New York: Holt, 1978.

Smith, Mark Edward. "Peer Tutoring in a Writing Workshop." Ph.D. dissertation, Univeristy of Michigan, 1976.

Smith, Vernon H. "Measuring Teacher Judgment in the Evaluation of Written Composition." *Research in the Teaching of English* 3 (1969): 181-195.

Smitherman, Geneva. *Talkin and Testifyin: The Language of Black America.* Boston: Houghton Mifflin, 1977.

Snow, Jerry J. "What Works and What Doesn't: Developmental Education in the Community College." Mimeographed. Austin, Tex.: University of Texas, 1977.

Snow, Jerry J., et al. "Tutorial Assistance Program Evaluation: Impact and Effectiveness." Austin, Tex.: Dean of Students Office, University of Texas, 1975.

Stalker, James. "A Linguist's View of the Composing Process." *CEA Critic* 40 (1978): 15-23.

Steiner, Karen. "Selected Bibliography of Individualized Approaches to College Composition: An ERIC/RCS Report." *College Composition and Communication* 28 (1977): 232-234.

Strong, William. *Sentence Combining: A Composing Book.* New York: Random House, 1973.

Selected Bibliography

Sullins, W. Robert, and Charles A. Atwell. "The Desired Preparation of English Teachers as Perceived by Community College Administrators." Unpublished essay, Virginia Polytechnic Institute, 1978.

Tate, Gary, ed. *Teaching Composition: Ten Bibliographical Essays.* Fort Worth, Tex.: Texas Christian University Press, 1976.

Thomas, Lucille M. *The Relevance of Patterns.* Sunnyvale, Calif.: Westinghouse Learning Corp., 1976.

Thorndike, Robert L., ed. *Educational Measurement.* 2nd ed. Washington, D. C.: American Council on Education, 1971.

Tolson, Henrietta. "Counseling the Disadvantaged." *Personnel and Guidance Journal* 50 (1972): 735-738.

Underwood, Virginia, and Merriellyn Kett. *Writing Skills.* Columbus, Ohio: Charles E. Merrill, 1977.

Van Bruggen, John A. "Factors Affecting Regularity of the Flow of Words during Written Composition." *Journal of Experimental Education* 15 (1946): 133-155.

Warnock, John. "New Rhetoric and the Grammar of Pedagogy." *Freshman English News* 5 (1976): 1-4, 12-22.

Weddington, Doris Clinard. *Patterns for Practical Communications: Composition.* Englewood Cliffs, N. J.: Prentice-Hall, 1976.

Weddington, Doris Clinard. *Patterns for Practical Communications: Sentences.* Englewood Cliffs, N. J.: Prentice-Hall, 1976.

Weddington, Doris Clinard. "Taped Feedback—Have You Tried It?" *Journal of Developmental and Remedial Education* 1 (1978): 10-11, 18.

West, Leonard J. *300 Commas.* New York: McGraw-Hill, 1964.

Witkin, H. A. *The Role of Cognitive Style in Academic Performance and in Teacher-Student Relations.* Princeton, N. J.: Educational Testing Service, 1973.

Witkin, H. A., and C. A. Morre. *Field Dependent and Field Independent Cognitive Styles and Their Educational Implications.* Princeton, N. J.: Educational Testing Service, 1975.

Wolff, Robert Lee, chair. *Report of the Committee on the Future of the Graduate School.* Cambridge, Mass.: Faculty of Arts and Sciences, Harvard University, 1969.

Worth, George J. "Reviewing the Graduate Curriculum: Opportunities and Obligations." *ADE Bulletin* 56 (1978): 2.

Wright, E. L. "Student and Instructor Perceptions of Developmental Program Instructors as a Function of Personal Characteristics in Selected Community Colleges in Texas." Ph.D. dissertation, University of Texas at Austin, 1975.

Wylie, Ruth C. *The Self-Concept: A Review of Methodological Considerations and Measuring Instruments.* Vol. 1. Lincoln: University of Nebraska Press, 1974.

Yarington, David J. *The Great American Reading Machine.* Rochelle Park, N. J.: Hayden, 1977.

Young, Charles E., and Emil F. Symonik. *Practical English.* New York: McGraw-Hill, 1975.

Zoellner, Robert. "Talk-Write: A Behavioral Pedagogy for Composition." *College English* 30 (1969): 267-320.

Notes

Chapter One

1. K. Patricia Cross, *Accent on Learning* (San Francisco: Jossey-Bass, 1976), p. 24.
2. John Roueche and Charles Wheeler, "Instructional Procedures for the Disadvantaged," *Improving College and University Teaching* 21 (1973): 223.
3. Cross, *Accent on Learning*, p. 31.
4. Ibid.
5. See the following: Richard M. Bossone and Lynn Q. Troyka, *A Strategy for Coping with High School and College Remedial English Problems* (New York: Center for Advanced Studies in Education, 1976); Bossone and Max Weiner, *City University English Teachers: A Self-Report Regarding Remedial Teaching* (New York: CUNY Graduate School and University Center, 1975); Edmund W. Gordon, *Opportunity Programs for the Disadvantaged in Higher Education* (Washington, D.C.: American Association for Higher Education, 1975); Gordon, "Toward Defining Equality of Educational Opportunity," *On Equality of Educational Opportunity*, ed. F. Mosteller and Daniel P. Moynihan (New York: Random House, 1972); Gordon and Doxey Wilkerson, *Compensatory Education for the Disadvantaged* (New York: College Entrance Examination Board, 1966); Mary Janet Mulka and Edmund J. Sheerin, *An Evaluation of Policy-Related Research on Postsecondary Education for the Disadvantaged*, 2 vols. (Washington, D.C.: National Science Foundation, 1974); James Coleman et al., *Equality of Educational Opportunity* (Washington, D.C.: U.S. Government Printing Office, 1966); John Roueche and R. Wade Kirk, *Catching Up: Remedial Education* (San Francisco: Jossey-Bass, 1973); Roueche and Jerry J. Snow, *Overcoming Learning Problems* (San Francisco: Jossey-Bass, 1977).
6. Mulka and Sheerin, *Research on Postsecondary Education for the Disadvantaged*, p. 94.
7. I. Katz, "Academic Motivation and Equal Educational Opportunity," *Harvard Educational Review* 33 (1968): 57-65.
8. A. J. Jaffe and Walter Adams, *Academic Socio-Economic Factors Related to Entrance and Retention at Two- and Four-Year Colleges in the Late 60's* (Washington, D.C.: Bureau of Applied Social Resources, Office of Education, DHEW, 1970).
9. John Folger et al., *Human Resources and Higher Education* (New York: Russell Sage Foundation, 1970), p. 319.
10. Gordon and Wilkerson, *Compensatory Education*, p. 11.
11. Roueche and Kirk, *Catching Up*, p. 69. Also see Coleman et al. *Educational Opportunity*, pp. 367-445.
12. Coleman et al., *Educational Opportunity*, p. 325.

13. Cross, *Accent on Learning*, p. 34.

14. Mina Shaughnessy, *Errors and Expectations: A Guide for the Teacher of Basic Writing* (New York: Oxford University Press, 1977), p. 14.

15. E. Donald Hirsch, Jr., *The Philosophy of Composition* (Chicago: University of Chicago Press, 1977); Walter J. Ong, S.J., "Literacy and Orality in Our Times," *ADE Bulletin* 58 (September 1978): 1-7.

16. See William Labov, *The Study of Nonstandard English* (Urbana, Ill.: NCTE, Center for Applied Linguistics, and ERIC, 1970); Roger Shuy, *Field Techniques in an Urban Language Study* (Washington, D.C.: Center for Applied Linguistics, 1968); and Walter Wolfram, "The Nature of Non-Standard Dialect Divergence," in *Research Bases for Oral Language Instruction*, ed. Thomas Horn (Urbana, Ill.: NCTE, 1971).

17. Benjamin S. Bloom, "Mastery Learning," in *Mastery Learning: Theory and Practice*, ed. J. H. Block (New York: Holt, 1971); Bloom, *Handbook on Formative and Summative Evaluation of Student Learning* (New York: McGraw-Hill, 1971).

18. Jasper P. Neel and Jeanne C. Nelson, "From the Editor," *ADE Bulletin* 56 (February 1978): i-iii.

19. George J. Worth, "Reviewing the Graduate Curriculum: Opportunities and Obligations," *ADE Bulletin* 56 (February 1978): 2.

20. Kenneth A. Bruffee, "A New Intellectual Frontier," *Chronicle of Higher Education*, 27 February 1978, p. 40.

Chapter Two

1. Janet Emig, "Components of the Composing Process among Twelfth-Grade Writers" (Ph.D. diss., Harvard University, 1969). Janet Emig, *The Composing Processes of Twelfth Graders*, Research Report No. 13 (Urbana, Ill.: NCTE, 1971); Donald Graves, "Children's Writing: Research Directions and Hypotheses Based upon an Examination of the Writing Process of Seven Year Old Children" (Ph.D. diss., State University of New York at Buffalo, 1973).

2. Emig, *Composing Processes*, p. 1.

3. Ibid., p. 4.

4. Ibid., pp. 34-35.

5. Ibid., p. 91.

6. Ibid., p. 97.

7. Ibid., p. 98.

8. Graves, "Children's Writing," pp. 212-213.

9. Sondra Perl, "Five Writers Writing: Case Studies of the Composing Processes of Unskilled College Writers" (Ph.D. diss., New York University, 1978); see also Perl, *Coding the Composing Process* (Washington, D.C.: National Institute of Education, forthcoming).

10. As part of the Libra program, writing teachers attend the content course. In this way, the writing teacher can base writing instruction on "content" or conceptual issues students are studying; and students can come to recognize that writing is not an isolated skill but a language process used to convey and extend knowledge in all fields.

11. Richard Bossone and Max Weiner, *City University English Teachers:*

A Self-Report Regarding Remedial Teaching (New York: CUNY Graduate School and University Center, 1975), p. 19.

12. Mina Shaughnessy, *Errors and Expectations: A Guide for the Teacher of Basic Writing* (New York: Oxford University Press, 1977), p. 5.

13. For an extended discussion of the implications of these hypotheses for both theory and classroom practice, see Sondra Perl and Arthur Egendorf, "The Process of Creative Discovery: Theory, Research, and Implications for Teaching," in *Linguistics, Stylistics, and the Teaching of Composition*, ed. Donald McQuade (Akron, Ohio: L & S Books, forthcoming).

14. Shaughnessy, *Errors and Expectations*, p. 49.

15. Ibid., p. 172.

Chapter Three

1. See, for example, Charles R. Cooper, "Holistic Evaluation of Writing," in *Evaluating Writing: Describing, Measuring, Judging*, eds. Charles R. Cooper and Lee Odell (Urbana, Ill.: NCTE, 1977), pp. 3-31.

2. Nonstandard forms are found among many ethnic and regional groups, of course, and there are similarities in the forms and occurrence from group to group. See Mina Shaughnessy, *Errors and Expectations: A Guide for the Teacher of Basic Writing* (New York: Oxford University Press, 1977), pp. 91-93. See also pages 157 ff. on contrastive analysis in teaching standard dialect.

3. Shaughnessy, *Errors and Expectations*, p. 153. Also, William Labov, *The Study of Nonstandard English* (Urbana, Ill.: NCTE, Center for Applied Linguistics, and ERIC, 1970), pp. 35-36.

4. On the importance of self-image, see Mary Janet Mulka and Edmund J. Sheerin, *An Evaluation of Policy-Related Research on Postsecondary Education for the Disadvantaged* (Washington, D.C.: National Science Foundation, 1974), p. 66; A. J. Jaffe and Walter Adams, *Academic Socio-Economic Factors Related to Entrance and Retention at Two- and Four-Year Colleges in the Late 60's* (Washington, D.C.: Bureau of Applied Social Resources, Office of Education, DHEW, 1970), p. 9. On the importance of providing real achievement based on competence as well as positive personal feedback, see Mulka and Sheerin, *Research on Postsecondary Education for the Disadvantaged*, pp. 188, 236.

5. See Frank O'Hare, *Sentence Combining: Improving Student Writing without Formal Grammar Instruction*, Research Report No. 15 (Urbana, Ill.: NCTE, 1973), where the basic research is reviewed.

6. Donald Bateman and Frank Zidonis, *The Effect of a Study of Transformational Grammar on the Writing of Ninth and Tenth Graders*, Research Report No. 6 (Urbana, Ill.: NCTE, 1966).

Chapter Four

1. Doris Clinard Weddington, "Taped Feedback—Have You Tried It?" *Journal of Developmental and Remedial Education* 1 (1978): 10-11, 18.

2. Teresa Ferster Glazier, *The Least You Should Know about English* (New York: Holt, 1977); Robert R. Potter, *Language Workshop* (New York: Globe, 1976); Lucille M. Thomas, *The Relevance of Patterns* (Palo Alto: Westinghouse Learning Corp., 1973); Doris Clinard Weddington, *Patterns for Practical Communi-*

cations: Sentence (Englewood Cliffs, N.J.: Prentice-Hall, 1976); Charles E. Young and Emil F. Symonik, *Practical English* (New York: McGraw-Hill, 1975).

3. *Comparative Guidance and Placement Program, Form SPG* (Princeton: Educational Testing Service, 1970).

4. Betty McFarland, "The Non-Credit Writing Laboratory," *Teaching English in the Two-Year College* 1 (1975): 153-154. Also see McFarland's "Counterstatement," *Teaching English in the Two-Year College* 2 (1976): 179-180.

5. Instructional materials available in the laboratory include the following: Joseph C. Blumenthal, *English 2600*, 3rd ed. (New York: Harcourt Brace Jovanovich, 1970); Joseph C. Blumenthal, *English 3200*, 2nd ed. (New York: Harcourt Brace Jovanovich, 1972); Eugenia Butler, *An Auto-Instructional Text in Correct Writing*, 2nd ed. (Lexington, Mass.: D.C. Heath, 1976); *Educulture English Modular Mini-Courses*, Modules 1-17 (Santa Monica, Calif.: Educulture Tutorial Systems, 1973); Susan Fawcett, *Grassroots: The Writer's Workbook* (Boston: Houghton Mifflin, 1976); James Gowan, *English Review Manual* (New York: McGraw-Hill, 1970); John C. Hodges, *Harbrace College Handbook*, 5th ed. (New York: Harcourt Brace Jovanovich, 1962); James McCrimmon, *Writing with a Purpose*, 5th ed. (Boston: Houghton Mifflin, 1973); Porter G. Perrin, *Handbook of Current English*, 3rd ed. (Glenview, Ill.: Scott, Foresman, 1968); William Strong, *Sentence Combining: A Composing Book* (New York: Random House, 1973); Leonard J. West, *300 Commas* (New York: McGraw-Hill, 1964).

6. Betty McFarland, *Writing and Proofreading: Priority #4* (Boone, N.C.: Appalachian State University English Department, 1977). This publication consists of a model writing unit and five booklets on usage errors: fragments, run-on sentences, subject-verb disagreement, pronoun-antecedent disagreement, incorrect verb form.

7. *Sequential Tests of Educational Progress, Form 1B* (Princeton: Educational Testing Service).

8. For further information on this kind of course, see Betty McFarland, "An Individualized Course in Elementary Composition for the Marginal Student," in *Personalized Instruction in Higher Education: Proceedings of the Second National Conference*, ed. Ben A. Green, Jr. (1976), pp. 45-48. Also see "An Alternative Program for Basic Composition Courses," a paper presented by Betty McFarland at the 1978 Annual Meeting of the Southeastern Conference on English in the Two-Year College, available from the author.

9. David R. Krathwohl, Benjamin S. Bloom, and Bertram B. Masia, *Taxonomy of Educational Objectives* (New York: David McKay, 1974).

10. We wish to thank the following individuals who helped us with the preparation of this article: Betty McFarland, Appalachian State University; Libby Knowles, Appalachian State University; John Brame, Surry Community College; and Doris Weddington, Catawba Valley Technical Institute.

Chapter Five

1. See K. Patricia Cross, *Accent on Learning* (San Francisco: Jossey-Bass, 1976), chapter 4.

2. Thus I need to acknowledge the contributions of all those who worked with me in the laboratory, not only Robert H. Bentley, now at Lansing Community College, but also Fredrica K. Bartz, Mark K. Edmonds, and

Gregory Waters, the University of Michigan-Flint; Linda Bannister, now at the University of Southern California; Raymond Jaeger, now at Western Michigan University; and Arlette Smith, now at Rochester Community College.

3. See, for example, Anthony R. Petrosky, "Grammar Instruction—What We Know," *English Journal* 66 (1977): 86-89; W. B. Elley et al., "The Role of Grammar in a Secondary School English Curriculum," *Research in the Teaching of English* 10 (1976): 5-21; J. Stephen Sherwin, *Four Problems in Teaching English: A Critique of Research* (Scranton, Pa.: International Textbook Company, 1969), pp. 109-168; and Henry C. Meckel, "Research on Teaching Composition and Literature," in *Handbook of Research on Teaching*, ed. N. L. Gage (Chicago: Rand McNally, 1963).

4. See William Labov, "The Logic of Nonstandard English," in his *Language in the Inner City* (Philadelphia: University of Pennsylvania Press, 1972).

5. See, for one particular dialect, Labov, *Language in the Inner City;* Geneva Smitherman, *Talkin and Testifyin: The Language of Black America* (Boston: Houghton Mifflin, 1977); and, for an anthology specifically directed at teachers, Robert H. Bentley and Samuel D. Crawford, eds., *Black Language Reader* (Glenview, Ill.: Scott, Foresman, 1973).

6. Particularly Francis Christensen, with Bonniejean Christensen, *Notes toward a New Rhetoric*, 2nd ed. (New York: Harper and Row, 1978); Ken Macrorie, *Telling Writing*, 2nd ed. (New York: Hayden, 1976); and Robert Zoellner, "Talk-Write: A Behavioral Pedagogy for Composition," *College English* 30 (1969): 267-320.

7. Carol Chomsky, "Stages in Language Development and Reading Exposure," *Harvard Educational Review* 42 (1972): 1-33; Rita S. Brause, "Developmental Aspects of the Ability to Understand Semantic Ambiguity, with Implications for Teachers," *Research in the Teaching of English* 11 (1977): 39-48.

8. For reading theory, see Frank Smith, *Understanding Reading*, 2nd ed. (New York: Holt, 1978); for linguistics, see Labov, *Language in the Inner City*, and M. A. K. Halliday, "Talking One's Way In: A Sociolinguistic Perspective on Language and Learning," in *Problems of Language and Learning*, ed. Alan Davies (London: Heineman, 1975), pp. 8-25; for rhetoric, see Janet Emig, *The Composing Processes of Twelfth Graders*, Research Report No. 13 (Urbana, Ill.: NCTE, 1971); John Warnock, "New Rhetoric and the Grammar of Pedagogy," *Freshman English News* 5 (Fall 1976): 1-4, 12-22; and James L. Kinneavy, "The Relation of the Whole to the Part in Interpretation Theory and the Composing Process," in *Language and Style*, ed. Donald McQuade (Akron, Ohio: University of Akron Press, forthcoming).

9. Such readings included, in addition to those already cited, K. Patricia Cross, *Beyond the Open Door: New Students in Higher Education* (San Francisco: Jossey-Bass, 1971), and Thomas Kochman, "Cross-Cultural Communication: Contrasting Perspectives, Conflicting Sensibilities," *Florida FL Reporter* 9 (1971): 3-16, 53-54.

10. For an extended discussion of peer tutoring, see Kenneth Bruffee's contribution to this volume.

11. James Britton, in *Problems of Language and Learning*, ed. Alan Davies (London: Heineman, 1975), pp. 113-126, reports that John A. Van Bruggen found the rate of writing to be fastest in both very skilled and very unskilled

writers. See Van Bruggen, "Factors Affecting Regularity of the Flow of Words during Written Composition," *Journal of Experimental Education* 15, no. 2 (1946).

12. For a discussion of this phenomenon—passing the test without learning the material—see the Writing Across the Curriculum Project report *From Information to Understanding: What Children Do with New Ideas*, 2nd ed. (London: London University Institute of Education, 1973).

13. Several articles have discussed the use of the tape recorder in teaching composition; more significant is the recognition of reading aloud as a means of evaluating writing, as, for example, in E. D. Hirsch, Jr., *The Philosophy of Composition* (Chicago: University of Chicago Press, 1977), p. 162.

14. Several journalism workbooks offer raw data for news stories. See, for example, Fred Fedler, *Reporting for the Print Media* (New York: Harcourt Brace Jovanovich, 1973), and Melvin Mencher, *Workbook for News Reporting and Writing* (Dubuque, Iowa: William C. Brown, 1977).

15. Thomas J. Farrell, "Reading in the Community College," *College English* 37 (1975): 40-46.

16. See Christensen, "A Generative Rhetoric of the Paragraph," in his *Notes toward a New Rhetoric;* Robert M. Gorrell, "Not by Nature: Approaches to Rhetoric," *English Journal* 55 (1969): 409-416, 449; and Gorrell and Charlton Laird, *The Modern English Handbook*, 6th ed. (Englewood Cliffs, N.J.: Prentice-Hall, 1976), chapter 3.

17. The last suggested in Mark Lester, "The Value of Transformational Grammar in Teaching Composition," *College Composition and Communication* 18 (1967): 227-231.

18. See Patrick Hartwell, "The Great Punctuation Game," *Freshman English News* 6 (1979).

19. A useful tape-workbook for spelling is Odette P. Sims, *Spelling: Patterns of Sound* (New York: McGraw-Hill, 1974); a good programmed text is Patricia M. Fergus, *Spelling Improvement*, 2nd ed. (New York: McGraw-Hill, 1973).

20. The best approach to grammatical detail that I found when I was working in a laboratory situation was the tape-workbook program by Lucille M. Thomas, *The Relevance of Patterns* (Sunnyvale, Calif.: Westinghouse Learning Corp., 1976). Many of the exercises mentioned in my discussion have been incorporated in Patrick Hartwell and Robert H. Bentley, *Open to Language: A College Rhetoric* (New York: Oxford University Press, forthcoming). Suzette Haden Elgin offers a discovery approach to grammatical detail in "Don't No Revolutions Hardly *Ever* Come by Here," *College English* 39 (1978): 784-790. Model exercises in both grammatical detail and larger elements of structure are provided in Mina Shaughnessy, *Errors and Expectations: A Guide for the Teacher of Basic Writing* (New York: Oxford University Press, 1977).

21. Richard Ohmann, *English in America: A Radical View of the Profession* (New York: Oxford University Press, 1975), chapters 5 and 6.

22. R. P. McDermott, "Achieving School Failure: An Anthropological Approach to Illiteracy and Social Stratification," in *Theoretical Models and Processes of Reading*, ed. Harry Singer and Robert B. Ruddel, 2nd ed. (Newark, Del.: International Reading Association, 1976), p. 417.

Chapter Seven

1. K. Patricia Cross, *The Junior College Student: A Research Description* (Princeton: Educational Testing Service, 1968).

2. The topics were derived from Josephine Kehoe, "Compassionate Grading: Possible?" *Arizona English Bulletin* 16 (1974): 147-48.

3. B. D. M. Cast, "The Efficiency of Different Methods of Marking English Composition," *British Journal of Educational Psychology* 9 (November 1939): 257-269; 10 (February 1940): 49-60. Also see Ann F. Coward, "A Comparison of Two Methods of Grading English Compositions," *Journal of Educational Research* 46 (1952): 81-93; J. D. Nisbet, "English Composition in Secondary School Selection," *British Journal of Educational Psychology* 25 (February 1955): 51-54; Frances Ondee Ravan, "An Analytic Study of the Essay Test of the Language Skills Examination in the Georgia Rising Junior Testing Program" (Ed.D. diss., University of Georgia, 1973); Henry B. Slotnick, "An Examination of the Computer Grading of Essays" (Ph.D. diss., University of Illinois at Urbana-Champaign, 1971); Vernon H. Smith, "Measuring Teacher Judgment in the Evaluation of Written Composition," *Research in the Teaching of English* 3 (Fall 1969): 181-195.

4. Richard Braddock, Richard Lloyd-Jones, and Lowell Schoer, *Research in Written Composition* (Urbana, Ill.: NCTE, 1963). Also see Paul B. Diederich, "Grading and Measuring" (ERIC ED 031 479); Diederich, *Measuring Growth in English* (Urbana, Ill.: NCTE, 1974); and Fred Godshalk, Frances Swineford, and William E. Coffman, *The Measurement of Writing Ability* (New York: College Entrance Examination Board, 1966).

5. John Dewey, *Democracy and Education* (New York: Free Press, 1966), p. 165.

6. Ibid.

7. Thomas L. Green, *The Activities of Teaching* (New York: McGraw-Hill, 1971), p. 70.

8. Ibid.

9. John Galsworthy, "The Japanese Quince," in *Story and Structure*, ed. Laurence Perrine (New York: Harcourt Brace Jovanovich, 1974), p. 63.

10. John Bormuth, *On the Theory of Achievement Test Items* (Chicago: University of Chicago Press, 1970). Also see Norman Gronlund, *Constructing Achievement Tests* (Englewood Cliffs, N.J.: Prentice-Hall, 1968); Gronlund, *Measurement and Evaluation in Testing* (New York: Macmillan, 1971); and Robert L. Thorndike, ed., *Educational Measurement*, 2nd ed. (Washington, D.C.: American Council on Education, 1971).

11. Alan Purves et al., *Common Sense and Testing in English* (Urbana, Ill.: NCTE, 1975), p. 12.

12. Diederich, *Measuring Growth*, p. 101.

13. Ibid. See Kuder-Richardson Formula 20 or 21.

14. Gronlund, *Constructing Achievement Tests*.

15. For additional information concerning the N.V.C.C. Placement Test, see Nancy W. Johnson, "The Uses of Grammatical and Rhetorical Norms, Pedagogical Strategies and Statistical Methods in Designing and Validating a

Composition Placement Instrument" (Doctor of Arts diss., Catholic University of America, Washington, D.C., 1976).

Chapter Eight

1. O. K. Buros, ed., *The Seventh Mental Measurements Yearbook* (Edison, N.J.: Gryphon Press, 1972), pp. 465-502.
2. Rexford Brown, "Measuring Growth and Proficiency in Writing," *Journal of Basic Writing*, CCNY (Fall 1978).
3. Paul B. Diederich, "Cooperative Preparation and Rating of Essay Tests" (ERIC ED 091 750).
4. I. Mullis, *The Primary Trait System for Scoring Writing Tasks* (Denver: National Assessment of Educational Progress, 1976).
5. Edward Dixon, "Indexes of Syntactic Maturity" (ERIC ED 091 748).
6. John C. Mellon, "Factors of Syntactic Fluency" (ERIC ED 018 405).
7. Roy C. O'Donnell and Kellogg W. Hunt, "Syntactic Maturity," in *Measures for Research and Evaluation in the English Language Arts*, ed. William T. Fagan, Charles R. Cooper, and Julie M. Jensen (Urbana, Ill.: ERIC/RCS and NCTE, 1975), pp. 201-202.
8. Fritz P. Dauterman, "Syntactic Maturity Test for Narrative Writing" (ERIC ED 091 757).
9. Rexford Brown, *Writing Mechanics, 1969-1974* (Denver: National Assessment of Educational Progress, 1976).
10. Paul B. Diederich, *Measuring Growth in English* (Urbana, Ill.: NCTE, 1974).

Chapter Nine

1. W. Robert Sullins and Charles A. Atwell, "The Desired Preparation of English Teachers as Perceived by Community College Administrators" (Unpublished essay, Virginia Polytechnic Institute, 1978).
2. Two reports that describe the kinds of preparation desirable for community college teachers and for teachers of composition in general, including basic writing, are Eugene H. Smith, *Teacher Preparation in Composition* (Champaign, Ill.: NCTE and ERIC, 1969), and Gregory Cowan, *An Annotated List of Training Programs for Community College English Teachers: A CCCC Report* (Urbana, Ill.: ERIC/RCS, ERIC/JC, and CCCC, 1977). Other articles and monographs dealing with the subject of teacher preparation for basic writing are listed in week thirteen of the model syllabus described in this article.
3. A good illustration of the increasing awareness teachers have of the need for individualized instruction is Karen Steiner's "Selected Bibliography of Individualized Approaches to College Composition: An ERIC/RCS Report," *College Composition and Communication* 28 (1977): 232-234. Another is the two volumes published by the University of South Carolina at Columbia in 1977, the result of an NEH grant, which contain a variety of helpful articles for training tutors in individualized instruction: *The Writing Laboratory Report and Handbook*, vol. 1, *General Orientation*, ed. Larry Howland; and vol. 2, *Workshops*, ed. Steve Bannow.

4. Mina Shaughnessy, *Errors and Expectations: A Guide for the Teacher of Basic Writing* (New York: Oxford University Press, 1977), p. 6.

5. John A. Higgins, "Remedial Students' Needs vs. Emphases in Text-Workbooks," *College Composition and Communication* 24 (1973): 188.

6. Maureen Moment, "A Description of the Writing of English 1000 Students at Virginia Polytechnic Institute and State University" (M.A. thesis, Virginia Polytechnic Institute, 1978).

7. Ibid., p. 58.

8. Kellogg W. Hunt, *Grammatical Structures Written at Three Grade Levels*, Research Report No. 3 (Urbana, Ill.: NCTE, 1965), and John C. Mellon, *Transformational Sentence-Combining: A Method for Enhancing the Development of Syntactic Fluency in English Composition*, Research Report No. 10 (Urbana, Ill.: NCTE, 1969).

9. One of the best is John E. Roueche and Jerry J. Snow, *Overcoming Learning Problems* (San Francisco: Jossey-Bass, 1977).

10. Complete bibliographic information about all the books mentioned in this section is included in the course syllabus that follows.

11. Shaughnessy, *Errors and Expectations*, p. 5.

12. Ibid., pp. 9-11.

13. Ibid., p. 17.

14. Ibid., p. 26.

15. Ibid., p. 44.

16. Ibid., p. 49.

17. Bibliographic information is contained in the reading list for week seven.

18. See William Labov, *The Study of Nonstandard English* (Urbana, Ill.: NCTE, Center for Applied Linguistics, and ERIC, 1970), pp. 28-30, for a discussion of how the rules of a second dialect are incorporated into one's linguistic repertoire.

Chapter Ten

1. Although the program is of my own design, it owes its existence to the collaborative effort and vision of many people. I cannot possibly mention them all, but I must at least discharge my debt to Judy Fishman for her valuable suggestions in writing this essay.

2. The Nassau Community College program was designed and directed by Paula Beck. A program at Queens College directed by Judy Fishman is modeled in part on the Brooklyn program, but has valuable innovative features of its own.

A useful general description of a basic peer-tutoring program is Mark Edward Smith's dissertation, "Peer Tutoring in a Writing Workshop," University of Michigan (Ann Arbor, Mich.: Xerox University Microfilms, No. 76-9320, 1976). Besides practical advice, Smith also discusses the theoretical background of peer tutoring. A journal article discusses peer-tutoring programs at three very different institutions: Brooklyn College, Nassau Community College, and the University of California at Berkeley; see Paula Beck, Thom Hawkins, and Marcia Silver, "Training and Using Peer Tutors," *College English* 40 (1978): 432-449, and an article by Bruffee entitled "The Brooklyn Plan: Attaining Intellectual Growth Through Peer-Group Influence," *Liberal Education*, (1978): 447-468.

3. Sophie Bloom, *Peer and Cross-Age Tutoring in Schools* (Washington, D.C.: National Institute of Education, DHEW, 1976), pp. 17-18. This pamphlet is required reading for anyone starting or developing a peer-tutoring program.

4. Ibid.

5. Beck, Hawkins, and Silver, "Training and Using Peer Tutors." See also Mary H. Beaven, "Individualized Goal Setting, Self-Evaluation, and Peer Evaluation," in *Evaluating Writing: Describing, Measuring, Judging*, ed. Charles R. Cooper and Lee Odell (Urbana, Ill.: NCTE, 1977), pp. 148-53. Smith, "Peer Tutoring," has a chapter on evaluation that stresses the difficulties involved.

6. Two programs that emphasize the educational aspect of training peer tutors are those at Queens College and the University of California at Berkeley.

7. See E. D. Hirsch, Jr., *The Philosophy of Composition* (Chicago: University of Chicago Press, 1977), pp. 28-32.

8. The course normally uses as a text my own *A Short Course in Writing* 2d ed., (Cambridge, Mass.: Winthrop, 1972), although any text dealing with the basic elements of argumentative form in a practical way might do as well.

9. This procedure is described in detail in Bruffee, *A Short Course in Writing*, pp. 23f., 36-38.

10. Compare Silver's description of this process in Beck, Hawkins, and Silver, "Training and Using Peer Tutors," and *A Short Course in Writing*, pp. 103f., 208-215. The process is the basis of an Institute in Training Peer Tutors offered by Brooklyn College in Summer 1980-81, supported by FIPSE.

11. The discipline of social group work, especially in its less theoretical form as taught and practiced by William Schwartz of Columbia University Graduate School of Social Work, has a great deal to offer teachers who attempt to bring peer influence to bear on intellectual growth. A primer may be found in Schwartz's introduction to *The Practice of Group Work*, ed. William Schwartz and Serapio R. Zalba (New York: Columbia University Press, 1971), pp. 3-24.

12. Nevitt Sanford, ed., *The American College* (New York: Wiley, 1962), pp. 482-487. See also "The Organizational Context," in *College Peer Groups*, ed. Theodore M. Newcomb and Everett K. Wilson (Chicago: Aldine, 1966), p. 67; Robert Lee Wolff, chair, *Report of the Committee on the Future of the Graduate School* (Cambridge, Mass.: Faculty of Arts and Sciences, Harvard University, 1969); and Jerome Bruner, "The Uses of Immaturity," *Times Education Supplement* (London), 27 October 1972, reprinted in *Intellectual Digest*, February 1973. For a larger perspective on the need to involve undergraduates in their own education, see James S. Coleman et al., *Youth: Transition to Adulthood* (Washington, D.C.: Office of Science and Technology, 1973), especially p. 156; and Ann Kieffer Bragg, *The Socialization Process in Higher Education*, ERIC-American Association for Higher Education Report No. 7 (Washington, D.C.: American Association for Higher Education, 1976).

Contributors

Rexford Brown is Director of Publications of the National Assessment of Educational Progress. He has served as a consultant for numerous government bodies, colleges, and foundations. Brown has spoken frequently on the topic of testing in English and has contributed to seven books published by the National Assessment.

Kenneth A. Bruffee is Professor of English, Brooklyn College, City University of New York, and editor of the *WPA Newsletter*, a quarterly publication of the Council of Writing Program Administrators. His publications include *A Short Guide to Writing* and numerous journal articles on teaching writing.

Harry Crosby is Professor of English and Chairman, Department of Rhetoric, College of Basic Studies, Boston University. Previously, he served as Writing Supervisor at the University of Iowa. He has published six textbooks and a number of journal articles on the teaching of writing.

Arthur L. Dixon is Associate Professor of English at J. Sargeant Reynolds Community College. He previously taught English at Southern Illinois University.

Virginia Foxx is Assistant Dean of the General College and Coordinator for Developmental Studies, Appalachian State University. She has taught sociology at the University of North Carolina, Caldwell Community College, and Appalachian State.

Constance J. Gefvert is Associate Professor of English and Director of Freshman English, Virginia Polytechnic Institute and State University. She has taught at Wayne State University, the University of Minnesota, and Illinois State University. Her publications include papers on black English and, as coauthor, *Keys to American English*.

Patrick Hartwell is Associate Professor of English and Director of Freshman English at the University of Cincinnati. He previously taught at the University of Michigan-Flint and UCLA. His publications include journal articles on the teaching of writing and, as coauthor, the forthcoming *Open to Language: A College Rhetoric*.

E. Donald Hirsch, Jr., is Kenan Professor of English at the University of Virginia. He has published widely in the areas of literature, criticism, and rhetoric. His books include *Innocence and Experience: An Introduction to Blake, The Aims of Interpretation,* and *The Philosophy of Composition.*

Daniel R. Hoeber is Assistant Professor and Director of Writing, Mercy College, Detroit. Hoeber has designed, directed, and taught in basic writing programs at Southern Illinois University, Emmanuel County Community College, and Mercy College.

Nancy W. Johnson is Associate Professor of English, Northern Virginia Community College. She has spoken on the teaching of writing and on testing at a number of professional meetings.

Lawrence N. Kasden is Associate Professor and Chairman, Department of English, J. Sargeant Reynolds Community College. He has spoken on the topic of basic writing at many professional meetings and has recently published journal articles on the same subject.

Sondra Perl is Assistant Professor of English, Herbert H. Lehman College, City University of New York. She is Codirector of the Writing Development Project and Director of the New York City Writing Project. Her publications include *Coding the Composing Process.*

Milton G. Spann is Associate Professor and Director of the Center for Developmental Education, Appalachian State University. He has taught at several two- and four-year institutions and has published widely; he is presently editor of the *Journal of Developmental and Remedial Education.*

George Open   Ken Hunt

274- / 3000 [Ann Malone] — runs writing lab at Loyola

366-2490 [Smokey Daniels] — Rosary Coll. River Forest

[B.J. Wagner] — Nat'l call. — did stuff w/ Jim Moffett
student-centered Lang art
Teach'g the Univ. of Disc.

Bob Gundlach — N.U.

[Within Roos.]

Monday 15th

Friday 12th

(11:30)

Bread Shop Restaurant